The TSUNAMI Restaurant Cookbook

The TSUNAMI Restaurant Cookbook

By Ben Smith

PELICAN PUBLISHING COMPANY
GRETNA 2005

The word "Pelican" and the depiction of a pelican are trademarks of Pelican Publishing Company, Inc., and are registered in the U.S. Patent and Trademark Office.

Library of Congress Cataloging-in-Publication Data

Smith, Ben, 1962-
    The Tsunami restaurant cookbook / by Ben Smith.
        p. cm.
    Includes index.
    ISBN-13: 978-1-58980-282-7 (hardcover : alk. paper)
  1. Cookery, Asian. 2. Tsunami (Restaurant) I. Title.
    TX724.5.A1S55 2005
    641.595—dc22

                                                2005011414

Photographs by Ben Couvillion
Photograph on page 6 by Jim Kiihnl

Printed in Singapore

Published by Pelican Publishing Company, Inc.
1000 Burmaster Street, Gretna, Louisiana 70053

For Colleen

contents

acknowledgments

The success of a restaurant depends on many people. One of my most important accomplishments in opening Tsunami was to surround myself with individuals who make me look brilliant. That is a monumental task, I know, but they have done it. My staff has unquestioningly and unflaggingly assumed the responsibility of promoting my food philosophy. They have never failed me. I respect, love, and admire them all more than I can express in words. Thank you all.

My wife, Colleen, deserves individual recognition, as she is charged with the tiresome responsibility of dealing with me both at work, where she is my general manager, and at home, where she is also my general manager. She does a tremendous job on both fronts. Thanks, babe.

I want to thank my two sons, Brendan and Ian, who have learned to keep half of their toys at the restaurant, because they know full well that when Daddy says, "We need to stop by the restaurant for a minute," it usually means they will be stuck there for hours. Don't worry—before long you'll be washing dishes and doing prep work, and at least you will be getting paid for all those hours. Thanks, guys.

Thanks to my family, who has encouraged and supported me throughout the years, never once suggesting I "get a real job."

I appreciate that I have learned a lot about the business end of the restaurant from my business partner, Thomas Boggs. I thank him for putting his trust in my concept, even when it was sometimes at odds with his business sense.

My literary agent, Linda Konner, was able to see my vision for this book and encourage me in spite of my nearly nonexistent verbal skills. I thank her for that.

I would also like to express my deepest gratitude to those folks, too numerous to mention here, who have supported my restaurant with their continued patronage since we opened in 1998. Thanks to all of you, especially those who send a glass of wine back to the kitchen once in a while.

introduction

I have always been good about listening to the advice of people I trust and respect. Then I go off and do something completely different. This has done nothing to instill any sense of satisfaction in any of my many advisors. Nor, to the credit of said advisors, has it slowed them down in their advisory proclivities. However, when I opened my own restaurant, I may have given rise to some hope that I had finally done something with all that advice.

The truth is that I took that step simply because I could no longer work for anybody else. "Creative freedom" is an oxymoron as long as somebody else is the boss. As a chef, I grew weary of the endless stream of suggestions from restaurant owners, some of whom were very good businessmen, but none of whom were very good menu planners. I came to a point where I refused to make any more recipes clipped out of *Southern Ladies' Home Kountry Kitchen Garden Journal*, or ensure that all my dinner specials have "sauce, and plenty of it," or create a "romantic dinner for two" including a bottle of wine for under twenty-five dollars (with coupon). All of that went against my principal belief that a restaurant should clearly represent the chef's philosophy on food. I wanted to cook for people who came in for the food, not for people who came in for the "two-for-one" deal.

Tsunami opened in Memphis in July of 1998. This book represents a portfolio of my work since then. Like any body of work, it reflects influences and interpretations from my travels, work experiences, and interactions with numerous people along the way. Opening a Pacific Rim-inspired restaurant in the heart of the "barbecue belt" has not been without its challenges. From the very beginning I decided that Tsunami would serve the kind of food that I enjoy cooking and eating. I did not want to compromise my vision of food and ambience in order to appeal to a broader group of diners. I have stuck with that principle and, as a result, have achieved my dream job. Tsunami has attracted a staff and a clientele that are motivated by the same flavors and presentations that I enjoy.

I prefer clean, uncluttered presentations. I like crisp, identifiable flavors. I believe that ingredients should be allowed to speak for themselves. A good chef is merely the catalyst that helps transform a combination of ingredients into a dish that is greater than the sum of its parts. Presentation is a very important part of the dining experience. A plate consisting of only three elements speaks more to me than a plate towering with food and garnishes. Perhaps I have been overly influenced by my artist father, but I believe in *negative space* on a plate. In other words, what *isn't* there is just important as what *is* there.

Most of the photographs in this book were taken with a fifty-year-old Rolleiflex TLR camera using natural light in the dining room at Tsunami. All of the dishes were photographed directly out of the kitchen within minutes of being plated. No team of food stylists had their hands on any plate. No smoke and mirrors were utilized to produce these pictures. What you see is what you get. My point is that by following these recipes, there is no reason why you cannot get the same results at home.

The TSUNAMI Restaurant Cookbook

tools of
the trade

We wouldn't get very far in the kitchen without certain timesaving devices. Here are some tools I have found indispensable in preparing the recipes in this book.

'Tis an ill cook that cannot lick his own fingers.

—William Shakespeare

In her book *Cook's Tools: The Complete Manual of Kitchen Implements and How to Use Them*, Susan Campbell lists *hands* before any other tool in the kitchen. I would concur with her opinion that hands are the most important "tool" in the realm of food preparation. Where would we be without hand-tossed pizzas, hand-roll sushi, or finger food? In a professional kitchen, the hands take on multiple tasks. We chefs test the doneness of meat with our sense of touch. We use our cupped hands as measuring spoons. Our fingers are trained to pick up just the right amount of salt for the sauce we are reducing in a pan. And yes, we taste with our fingers.

In the often-chaotic circumstances under which we work, we don't always have the tools at hand that we need. But we do, thank goodness, have our hands at hand. Many is the time that a chef has had to sacrifice the first couple of layers of skin on his hand to pull a hot pan off of the stove. Every chef I know has used his or her hands as tongs to flip sizzling cuts of meat on the grill. And chefs are legendary for their ability to hold plates that are so hot that no other mortal can touch them (much to the dismay of servers the world over).

It is important for those of us who cook to realize that there was a time when food processors, spice grinders, blenders, and cappuccino machines did not exist. While all of these pieces of equipment are great conveniences and timesavers, not one of them (except perhaps the cappuccino machine) is indispensable. Everything that those modern machines of convenience can do, we can do with our own hands and a knife—which happens to be the next most important tool in the kitchen.

The invention of the first cutting tool, however crude, probably advanced the art of cooking more than any other invention since. In the twenty years that I have been cooking, I have collected numerous knives and lost many more. However, there are only four knives that I use on a frequent basis, and those are the knives I would recommend to anyone. With these knives you will be able to perform just about any cutting task in the kitchen.

Chef's knife: This is the most utilized knife in the kitchen. I have been using my Culinary Institute of America-issued chef's knife since 1984 for everything from cutting meat and fish, to chopping herbs, to opening bottles of beer.

Paring knife: This is one of the best tools for peeling garlic and ginger, paring fruits and vegetables, and other small cutting jobs. I buy inexpensive paring knives by the dozen at restaurant supply stores so that I always have several on hand.

Chinese cleaver: This is my favorite all-around knife. The Chinese cleaver (as opposed to a meat cleaver) is a great tool for chopping garlic, ginger, and herbs; mincing fish or meat; and pounding out cuts of meat or fish for *paillard* or carpaccio. The broad blade of the cleaver can be used as a sort of shovel to scoop up large amounts of chopped stuff. A pair of cleavers, one wielded in each hand, make short work of a pile of fresh herbs. Chinese cleavers can be found at Asian markets and are usually under ten dollars. The best ones are made of a solid piece of stainless steel. I still have the same pair of cleavers that I bought in San Francisco's Chinatown in 1986, and they serve me quite well.

Serrated bread knife: The serrated knife is good for more than just bread. It is great for peeling pineapples.

The most important factor in choosing the right knife for you is performance. Price does not always reflect quality. There is nothing a twenty-dollar paring knife can do that can't be done with a two-dollar paring knife. If that worn old knife that you inherited from your grandmother works for you, then there's no need to go out and buy an expensive new model. Having said that, there are some characteristics that all good knives have in common, such as a full tang, meaning that the knife is forged from one piece of metal to which a handle is attached. Good knives are also well balanced. Whatever knives you choose to outfit your kitchen with should be, more than anything, comfortable to handle. A good knife should feel right at home in your hand, not too heavy and not too light.

Along with owning knives comes the responsibility of taking care of them. Don't rely on someone else to keep your knives sharp. Invest in a good two- or three-sided sharpening stone and some honing oil, available at any hardware store. Learn how to sharpen a knife properly, and then do so on a regular basis. Sometimes you may have to trust your knives to an expert to get out the occasional nicks or gouges that occur. If you must get your knives professionally sharpened, make sure it is someone experienced with honing a knife and not just grinding it down on a belt sander.

Remember, a dull knife is more dangerous than a sharp one.

Here are three other tools that I heavily rely on in my trade. They should be invaluable to you too.

Mandoline: Next to knives, the mandoline is probably the most frequently used tool in my kitchen. While I love cutting things by hand, nothing matches the mandoline for speed and consistency. It is indispensable for slicing cabbage for slaw or julienning vegetables for salads. It is also good for thinly slicing ginger for easier chopping, or for thinly shaving onions.

Wok: If I could have only one cooking vessel in my kitchen, it would be a wok. There is nothing it can't do: stir-fry, steam, boil, poach, smoke, deep-fry, braise, sauté. Woks are reasonably priced and can be found in any Asian market and in most department stores. The best woks are hand-hammered out of a single piece of steel. The typical wok is bowl shaped, requiring a wok ring to hold it over your stove burner. Flat-bottomed woks work reasonably well, but the standard wok tools only work in a curved wok.

Grill: I think every household, however small, should have a grill. Entire books have been written on grilling, with whole chapters devoted to choosing the right grill. While there are nearly as many styles of grills as there are cars on the market, there are only two basic types: charcoal and gas. The fundamental question in deciding which type

of grill you should choose is this: are you a hands-on griller or a one-handed griller? If you enjoy the process of building a fire, anticipating the flames reaching just the right temperature, and banking the coals to create hot and cool spots, then you are definitely a charcoal-grill person. If, on the other hand, you like to grill with one hand so you can have a beer in the other hand, you're probably a gas-grill person. Not that there is anything wrong with having a beer while you work the grill, mind you. It's just that a beer tastes a lot better when you have worked up a little bit of a sweat first.

When choosing a grill, make sure it is the right size for your needs. If you grill for two people most of the time, you don't need to fire up a barrel-sized grill every time you cook out. Likewise, if you more often cook for a bigger group of folks, a small grill just won't cut it. Make sure your grill has a lid, so you can smoke foods and control flareups.

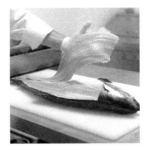

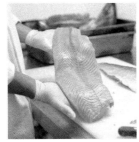

starters

Most of the recipes in this chapter can be picked up and eaten with one hand, making them ideal tidbits for backyard barbecues, cocktail parties, or any other informal get-together.

Clockwise from left: Ahi Poke, Tako Poke, Lomi Lomi Salmon

Satay Marinade

Satay, the quintessential Southeast Asian street food, has gained popularity around the world. It is one of the best ways to get a backyard barbecue going. As long as these are coming off the grill, you'll have no problem getting someone to bring you another cold beer.

½ cup peanut oil

1 stalk fresh lemongrass, minced (see sidebar)

3 cloves garlic, minced

½ tsp. crushed red pepper

1 tsp. Madras curry powder

1 tsp. Thai fish sauce

1 tsp. sugar

Mix all ingredients together until well blended. Makes enough for 1 lb. meat or vegetables.

Lemongrass

A perennial grass that is native to Southeast Asia, lemongrass adds remarkable fragrance and a pronounced lemon flavor to a dish without the acidity. It is an integral ingredient in many Thai and Vietnamese dishes. Readily available both fresh and dried in Asian markets, it is increasingly available in regular supermarkets as well. Many Asian markets stock already chopped lemongrass in the freezer section. While the frozen product is convenient, especially if you use a lot of it, there is no comparison to the wonderful aroma of freshly cut lemongrass.

Look for fresh stalks of lemongrass that are pale green turning to white at the bulb. The white bulb can be minced and used in dishes, or the stalks can be split and smashed before being added to sauces or soups and removed or strained out before serving. Lemongrass will keep well in the refrigerator for about two weeks.

Chicken Satay

5 boneless, skinless chicken breasts

1 recipe Satay Marinade

Cut each chicken breast into 3 long strips. Toss the strips in a bowl with the Satay Marinade until well coated. Allow to marinate for 8 hours or overnight.

Soak bamboo skewers in water for half an hour to keep them from catching fire on the grill. Skewer the chicken pieces lengthwise, then grill them over a medium-hot fire. Serve with Thai Peanut Sauce (see index). **Makes 15 satays.**

Shrimp Satay

2 lb. medium shrimp, peeled and deveined

Double recipe Satay Marinade

Toss the shrimp in the marinade in a bowl until well coated. Allow to marinate for 8 hours or overnight.

Skewer the shrimp (2 per stick) lengthwise on bamboo skewers that have been soaked in water for half an hour. Grill over a medium-hot fire. Serve with Thai Peanut Sauce or Thai Dipping Sauce with Cucumber and Peanuts (see index). **Makes about 24 satays.**

Beef Satay

1 flank steak

Double recipe Satay Marinade

Slice the flank steak across the grain into thin strips. (On a flank steak, the grain runs lengthwise, so cut across the width of the steak.) Toss the meat strips in a bowl with the marinade until well coated. Allow to marinate for 8 hours or overnight.

Thread the steak strips onto bamboo skewers that have been soaked in water for half an hour. Grill over a medium-hot fire. Serve with Thai Peanut Sauce (see index). **Makes about 20 satays.**

Curried Vegetable Egg Rolls

Egg rolls are great do-ahead appetizers for any get-together. An electric wok is a good alternative to a stovetop fryer. If you don't have an electric wok, use a regular wok or a thick-bottomed pot on the stove. Use a candy thermometer to check the temperature of the oil.

1 small clove garlic

1 tsp. chopped cilantro "chives" (cilantro stems)

1 tsp. peanut oil

1 tsp. ground black pepper

3 oz. sweet potato, peeled and minced

1 medium yellow onion, minced

1 large carrot, minced

2 tsp. Madras curry powder

1 tbsp. soy sauce

1 tsp. sugar

Salt to taste

12 egg-roll wrappers

1 small zucchini, julienned

1 small yellow squash, julienned

½ red bell pepper, julienned

2 tbsp. flour mixed with 2 tbsp. cold water to make a "slurry"

Peanut oil for frying

Chop the garlic and the cilantro "chives" together to make a paste. Preheat a skillet, add 1 tsp. peanut oil, and sauté the paste until aromatic, about 30 seconds. Add the black pepper, sweet potato, onion, carrot, and curry powder. Cook, stirring frequently, until the potatoes and carrots are soft. Season with the soy sauce, sugar, and salt. Remove from heat and cool completely.

To make the egg rolls, lay out 4 wrappers at a time on a clean, dry surface. Think of the wrapper as a baseball diamond. Place about 1 tbsp. filling in the middle of each wrapper just below the pitcher's mound. Spread out the filling so that it stretches to within 2 inches of first base and third base. Lay some of the julienned vegetables on top of the filling. Fold the home-plate corner over the filling and begin rolling the wrapper into a tight cylinder towards second base. When you reach the halfway point, fold in the first- and third-base corners. Keep rolling towards second base until only a tiny bit of the corner is showing. Using your fingertip, dab the corner with a little bit of the slurry and continue rolling to seal. Place the egg rolls on a cookie sheet lined with a clean, dry towel until they are all rolled.

To cook the egg rolls, preheat the peanut oil to 350 degrees in an electric wok or in a sturdy pot on the stovetop. If you don't have a thermometer, test the oil by sticking a bamboo or wooden chopstick into it. The chopstick should sizzle slightly when the oil is hot enough. Very carefully place the egg rolls into the hot oil. Fry them, 4 at a time, until golden brown. Remove to a cookie sheet lined with absorbent paper and keep them warm for a few minutes in a 300-degree oven. Serve with Nuoc Cham dipping sauce (see index). **Makes 12 egg rolls.**

Pork and Shrimp Lumpia

Lumpia is the Filipino version of the egg roll.

½ lb. green cabbage, chopped

1½ tsp. kosher salt

1 lb. ground pork

1 tbsp. chopped ginger

1½ tbsp. soy sauce

1½ tbsp. sesame oil

½ lb. small shrimp, peeled

1 large carrot, peeled and cut into matchstick-sized pieces (use a mandoline if you have one)

1 medium yellow onion, peeled, cut in half through the root, and sliced thin

Salt and pepper to taste

1 pkg. egg-roll wrappers

2 tbsp. flour mixed with 2 tbsp. water to make a "slurry"

Sprinkle the cabbage with the kosher salt and allow to sit in a colander for 10 minutes. Drain and squeeze out excess water. Place the cabbage in a bowl and add the ground pork, ginger, soy sauce, sesame oil, and shrimp. In a large skillet, cook the pork and shrimp mixture until the shrimp are cooked through. Add the carrots and onions and continue cooking until the carrots are al dente. Season with salt and pepper and cool the filling before rolling your lumpia.

To make the lumpia, lay out 4 or 5 wrappers at a time on a clean, dry surface. Think of the wrapper as a baseball diamond. Place about 2 oz. filling in the middle of each wrapper just below the pitcher's mound. Spread out the filling so that it stretches to within 2 inches of first base and third base. Fold the home-plate corner over the filling and begin rolling the lumpia into a tight cylinder towards second base. When you reach the halfway point, fold in the first- and third-base corners. Keep rolling towards second base until only a tiny bit of the corner is showing. Using your fingertip, dab the corner with a little bit of the slurry and continue rolling to seal.

Place the lumpia on a cookie sheet lined with a clean, dry towel until they are all rolled. Follow the instructions for frying Curried Vegetable Egg Rolls. Serve with Nuoc Cham dipping sauce (see index). **Makes about 25 lumpia.**

Spicy Chicken Lumpia

1 lb. boneless, skinless chicken breasts, diced

2 tbsp. sambal

1 tbsp. soy sauce

4 green onions, green part only, sliced

Egg-roll wrappers

Peanut oil for frying

Place the diced chicken in a food processor along with the sambal (see page 87) and soy sauce. Pulse until the chicken is the consistency of ground beef. Remove from the food processor and fold in the green onions by hand.

Lay out 4 or 5 wrappers on a clean, dry surface, add 1 heaping tbsp. filling to each, and follow the same rolling procedure as in the Pork and Shrimp Lumpia recipe. These lumpia are a much thinner version, about the circumference of a cigar, so they will cook rather quickly. Fry the lumpia until golden brown in peanut oil that has been preheated to around 350 degrees. **Makes 12-15 lumpia.**

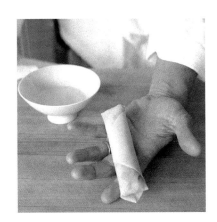

Crispy Calamari with Chipotle Aioli

People are always amazed to sample tender fried calamari. There's really no great mystery about cooking calamari. Just don't cook it too long. This flash-fried version is served with a spicy smoked chile and garlic mayonnaise, a nice alternative to the marinara sauce usually served with fried calamari.

3½ oz. canned chipotles in *adobo* (see sidebar)

2 egg yolks

1 clove garlic, minced

Juice of 1 lime

1 tsp. salt

1 cup olive oil

2 cups all-purpose flour

1 tsp. cayenne pepper

2 tsp. chili powder

2 tsp. salt

1 lb. small calamari, tubes and tentacles, cleaned

Peanut oil for frying

Lime wedges

Puree the chipotles in a blender until smooth. Add the egg yolks, garlic, lime juice, and salt and puree together until mixed. With the machine running, slowly drizzle in the olive oil until it is incorporated into the sauce. The sauce should have the consistency of mayonnaise.

Sift together the flour, cayenne pepper, chili powder, and salt in a large bowl. Make sure the calamari tentacles are free of any beaks and the tubes are thoroughly cleaned. Leave the tentacles whole and cut the tubes into rings about 1 inch wide.

Preheat the peanut oil to 350 degrees in an electric wok or in a stovetop fryer. Just before cooking, put half of the calamari into the bowl with the seasoned flour and toss it with your hands until it is well coated. Very gently drop the calamari into the hot oil and fry until just crisp. Using a wire-meshed scoop, remove the calamari to a platter lined with absorbent paper. Repeat with the remaining calamari. Serve immediately with the sauce and wedges of fresh lime for squeezing over the crispy calamari. **Serves 4.**

Chipotle Chiles

The chipotle is one of my all-time favorite chile peppers. Chipotles are jalapeños that have been dried and smoked. They add a marvelous smoky, spicy flavor to dishes. Dried chipotles are dark brown and quite wrinkled. They are also available pickled or canned in adobo *sauce. The dried version can be found in Latin markets and the canned version is often available in supermarkets in the Latin section. Dried chipotles need to be reconstituted in warm water before using (save the liquid and incorporate it into the final dish). Canned chipotles in* adobo *sauce can be pureed and used in anything from marinades and vinaigrettes to soups and sauces. Leftover chipotles in* adobo *sauce can be sealed in an airtight container and kept in the refrigerator for several weeks, which is a good thing, because a little goes a long way.*

Ahi Poke

Poke (pronounced po-kee) is a long-standing tradition in Hawaii. Ask ten different locals and you will get ten or twelve (or more!) different recipes. While ahi (yellowfin or bigeye tuna) is probably the most popular basis for poke, many different fish are used in this same preparation. Even tofu can be used in place of fish to create a vegetarian version. Just as the terms "julienne" and "dice" refer to certain types of cuts, in Hawaii, "poke" means "cut" or "cut crosswise." The key to any poke recipe is using the absolute freshest seafood you can find.

1 lb. of the freshest sushi-grade yellowfin tuna you can get your hands on

1 medium cucumber, peeled, seeded, and diced small

½ cup chopped green onions

3 tbsp. soy sauce

1 tsp. sesame oil

½ tsp. crushed red pepper

Juice of 1 lemon

Trim the tuna of any sinew or bloodline. Dice the tuna into small, pea-sized cubes and place in a stainless-steel or glass bowl. Add the remaining ingredients and toss together gently. Keep well chilled until ready to serve. In order to maintain the rich, red color of the tuna, serve as soon as possible after adding the liquid ingredients. You may assemble all of the ingredients ahead of time and then toss in the tuna right before serving. **Serves 4 to 6 as an hors d'oeuvre.**

Tako Poke

This recipe was given to me by my friend Al ("Tako Man") Alboro in Lanai City, Hawaii. (*Tako* is Japanese for octopus.) Al was an avid octopus hunter and was well known on the island of Lanai for this version of marinated octopus salad.

16 oz. beer

2 qt. water

1½-2 lb. fresh or previously frozen octopus, cleaned

1 bunch green onions, sliced

6 oz. sesame oil

1 tbsp. crushed red pepper

3 tbsp. sea salt

3 tbsp. soy sauce

Juice of 1 lemon

Bring the beer and water to a boil in a medium stockpot. Once the water is at a rolling boil, gently dip the octopus in until the tentacles begin to curl up. Remove the octopus and allow the water to come back to a boil. Repeat twice more. If you were to throw the octopus into the water all at once, the temperature would drop too suddenly. This gives the octopus a little head start in the cooking process while maintaining the proper temperature of the cooking liquid.

Allow the liquid to again return to a boil, and then add the entire octopus. Return to a boil, reduce to a bare simmer, and cook for 35-45 minutes. Remove from the heat and allow the octopus to cool in the liquid. Remove the octopus and cut the legs into thin "medallions" or slices. Place the octopus slices in a stainless-steel or glass bowl and add the remaining ingredients. Mix well and allow to marinate for several hours before serving. **Serves 6 as an hors d'oeuvre.**

Lomi Lomi Salmon

This dish is credited to Portuguese whalers who frequented Hawaii (then known as the "Sandwich Islands") in the early 19th century. This is a good example of early fusion cuisine. The Portuguese sailors adapted local ingredients and added them to a fish that they were more familiar with. In the Hawaiian language, *lomi lomi* means "rub" or "massage." Apparently, the motion of mixing all the ingredients by hand reminded the islanders of a massaging action, so the name Lomi Lomi Salmon stuck.

1 lb. very fresh salmon, cut into small cubes

4 tbsp. sea salt

6 roma tomatoes, seeded and diced

1 cup diced sweet onion (Vidalia or Maui)

4 green onions, sliced

In a stainless-steel or glass bowl, sprinkle the salmon with the sea salt and mix well to coat. Cover the salmon with cold water and place in the refrigerator overnight. Drain and rinse the salmon well in cold water. Add the tomatoes, sweet onion, and green onions and mix well with your hands. Serve well chilled with crispy fried won-ton chips (see Tuna Carpaccio recipe). **Serves 8 as an hors d'oeuvre.**

Tuna Sashimi

To me, there is no better way to eat tuna than raw with a little dab of wasabi and a splash of good-quality soy sauce. After a long, hot day in the kitchen this is often the only thing I am hungry for. Raw tuna has a much milder flavor than cooked tuna, which makes for a refreshing, clean taste. Wasabi adds that distinctive zing of intense heat; and the soy sauce satisfies my craving for saltiness. My mouth is watering as I write this.

1½-2 lb. very fresh sashimi-grade tuna

3 tbsp. wasabi powder dissolved in 3 tbsp. cold water

Finely shredded carrots

Finely shredded daikon radish

Soy sauce

Working on a clean, dry surface, cut the tuna into pieces about the size and shape of a domino. Fan the tuna slices out on a large platter. Place a dollop of wasabi paste in opposing corners. Garnish the platter with the vegetables. Serve with chopsticks and a shallow sauce dish full of soy sauce for each person.

Some people like to stir a little wasabi into the soy sauce before dipping the tuna. I prefer to smear a tad of the wasabi on each piece of tuna, top it with a bit of shredded daikon, and then dip it in the soy sauce. This requires a bit more dexterity with the chopsticks, but I think that a big part of the enjoyment of this dish is the mechanics involved with eating it. **Serves 4.**

Tuna Carpaccio with Wasabi Aioli, Pickled-Ginger Cream, and Daikon

Carpaccio originated in Italy and normally refers to thinly sliced raw beef garnished with olive oil, lemon, capers, and onions. This version of carpaccio uses raw tuna in the Italian style of presentation, but with traditional Japanese garnishes for sashimi. Even though I love the traditional beef, I find tuna carpaccio much more refreshing. This makes a dramatic presentation on a large platter.

2 lb. very fresh sashimi-grade yellowfin or bigeye tuna fillet in one piece

½ cup pickled ginger, drained and rinsed

2 tbsp. sour cream

¼ cup half-and-half

2 tbsp. water

2 tbsp. wasabi powder

1 tsp. minced garlic

Pinch salt

¾ cup olive oil

25-30 won-ton wrappers

Peanut oil for frying

½ cup finely grated daikon radish

Toasted sesame seeds

Shave the tuna *across* the fillet as thinly as possible. Think deli-meat thin. If you can't slice the tuna that thinly by hand, don't worry—there is another way. Slice the tuna no more than ¼ inch thick. Lay out the tuna slices between 2 sheets of plastic wrap. With a rolling pin, gently roll the tuna slices until they are paper thin. Remove the top layer of plastic wrap. The fish should stick to the bottom layer of wrap. Carefully invert this layer onto a chilled platter and peel it off, leaving the tuna on the platter. You can do the same thing for individual portions, only rolling a couple of slices of tuna at a time before transferring them to the chilled plates. Keep the tuna well chilled until you serve it.

Place the pickled ginger, sour cream, and half-and-half in a blender and puree until smooth. Stop the machine to scrape down the sides when necessary. Funnel the sauce into a plastic squeeze bottle and set aside.

In a small bowl, add the water to the wasabi powder and mix until smooth. Cover and set aside for 5 minutes to allow the flavor to develop. Add the minced garlic and a pinch of salt to the wasabi paste. Slowly drizzle in the olive oil while whisking. Funnel into a squeeze bottle.

Fry the won-ton wrappers in 1 inch peanut oil until crispy. Drain on absorbent paper and set aside.

Just before serving, squirt the pickled-ginger cream in a zigzag pattern across the platter (or the individual plates) of tuna. Do the same thing with the wasabi aioli. Garnish with a pile of grated daikon radish and toasted sesame seeds.

To eat, use a small fork to place a sliver of tuna onto a crispy won-ton chip. Top with a dollop of daikon radish. Eat. Repeat. **Serves 8.**

Scallop Ceviche

Although not cooked in the traditional sense, these scallops are rendered firm and opaque due to the action of the citrus juices. This technique of preserving fish is thousands of years old and originated in South America. Even though we no longer need to preserve fish in this manner, ceviche is still served today because it is so good. Only the freshest scallops will do for this dish.

½ cup lime juice

Juice of 2 lemons

1½ lb. very fresh sea scallops

¼ cup shaved red onion

1 tbsp. chopped cilantro

3 roma tomatoes, seeded and diced

2 tsp. olive oil

Salt to taste

Place the lime juice and lemon juice in a stainless-steel or glass bowl. Cut the scallops into cubes about the size of your thumbnail and add them to the citrus juices. Cover and refrigerate for 1 hour.

Drain the scallops and add the shaved red onion, cilantro, tomatoes, and olive oil. Season with salt. Serve in chilled martini glasses with tortilla chips. **Serves 6.**

Salmon Paillard with Crabmeat Beurre Blanc

Paillard is a term that usually refers to a very thin slice of meat that is quickly cooked. This hot appetizer consists of thin slices of salmon that are briefly broiled in the oven with crabmeat and topped with a beurre blanc sauce. The individual portions can be made up ahead of time and kept in the refrigerator until ready to cook.

1 tbsp. unsalted butter

1-1½ lb. salmon, sliced thin

½ lb. lump crabmeat, picked through for cartilage

1 tbsp. minced shallot

¼ cup dry white wine

¼ cup heavy whipping cream

½ lb. chilled unsalted butter, cut into ½-inch cubes

Salt and fresh-ground black pepper to taste

Chopped chives for garnish

Grease 6 ovenproof plates with the tablespoon of unsalted butter. Arrange the salmon slices evenly on each plate, overlapping slightly (3-4 oz. per plate). Sprinkle the crabmeat evenly over each plate. Place plates in a preheated 400-degree oven and bake 5-7 minutes or until salmon is opaque.

While the salmon is cooking, make the sauce. Place the shallot and white wine in a small saucepan and bring to a boil. Reduce the heat and simmer until the wine is nearly evaporated. Add the heavy cream, bring to a boil, and cook until the cream begins to thicken slightly. Whisk in the butter cubes one at a time until all the butter is incorporated into the sauce. Season to taste.

Remove the salmon from the oven, sauce each plate, garnish with chopped chives, and serve immediately. **Serves 6.**

Chipotle Shrimp with Mango Salsa

These spicy little snacks make a great pass-around hors d'oeuvre for a backyard barbecue or cocktail party. Everything can be made ahead, so all you have to do is put them together at the last minute.

1 can chipotles in *adobo*

Juice of 1 lime

2 lb. medium shrimp, peeled and deveined

40-50 good-quality tortilla chips

Chopped cilantro for garnish

Shredded lettuce or cabbage

Salsa

1 ripe mango, peeled, seeded, and diced small

Juice of 1 lime

2 tbsp. diced red bell pepper

2 green onions, sliced

½ bunch cilantro, chopped

1 tbsp. extra-virgin olive oil

Puree the chipotles in a blender with the lime juice. Pour half of the puree over the shrimp in a stainless-steel bowl. Reserve the remaining puree for another use. Marinate the shrimp for 2 hours.

To make the salsa, combine the mango, lime juice, pepper, onions, 2 tbsp. cilantro, and oil in a stainless-steel bowl. Mix well and keep the salsa in the refrigerator until ready to serve.

Lay the shrimp out on a baking sheet and cook in a preheated 350-degree oven for about 5 minutes or until the shrimp are cooked through. Remove from the oven and cool to room temperature. Place a spoonful of mango salsa on each tortilla chip and top with 1 shrimp. Garnish with chopped cilantro and serve on a platter lined with shredded lettuce or cabbage. **Makes about 50 hors d'oeuvre.**

Spice-Crusted Tuna
with Wasabi Aioli

This is an hors d'oeuvre version of one of our more popular entrees at Tsunami. There is a lot of flavor packed into one bite.

2 tsp. whole mustard seeds

1 tbsp. whole coriander

1 tsp. whole cumin seeds

2 tsp. kosher salt

1 lb. fresh tuna, cut into a long rectangle about 1 inch wide

2 tsp. olive oil

Wasabi Aioli

2 tbsp. wasabi powder

2 tbsp. cold water

2 egg yolks

½ tsp. minced garlic

¼ tsp. salt

½ tsp. rice vinegar

½ tsp. soy sauce

¼ tsp. sesame oil

1 cup olive oil

2 cucumbers, peeled and cut into ½-inch-thick rounds

Place the mustard seeds, coriander, and cumin in a dry, thick-bottomed skillet and toast the spices until they begin to smoke. Grind the spice blend in a coffee grinder or a mortar and pestle. Add the kosher salt and mix well. Spread the spice blend out on a plate and dredge the block of tuna in it until well coated on all sides.

Preheat a sauté pan, add olive oil, and briefly sear the tuna on all four sides, being careful to leave the tuna nice and rare on the inside. Remove from pan and cool to room temperature. Slice the tuna into squares about ¼ inch thick.

To make the aioli, in a small bowl, mix the wasabi powder with the water and stir until smooth. Invert the bowl and allow the wasabi paste to develop flavor for 5 minutes. Place the egg yolks, garlic, salt, vinegar, soy sauce, and sesame oil into a blender along with the wasabi paste. Place a small funnel in the top of the blender and with the machine running, slowly drizzle in the olive oil until it is incorporated and the sauce has the consistency of mayonnaise.

Place each slice of tuna on top of a slice of cucumber. Top with a small dollop of wasabi aioli. Serve immediately. **Makes 25-30 hors d'oeuvre.**

Wasabi

By now, most everyone is familiar with the spicy, green paste that garnishes every platter of sushi you order. Wasabi is actually the root of a perennial herb native to Japan that grows on the banks of cold, swift-moving streams. Wasabi is often referred to as "Japanese horseradish" although the two have no botanical relation. Fresh wasabi root is grated using a fine-toothed grater or sharkskin to produce a fine, pungent paste. Wasabi is an integral accompaniment to sushi and sashimi. Most of what passes for wasabi in America is actually a paste made from artificially colored mustard powder. It can be found in Asian markets and many supermarkets in both the premade paste form or in a powder, which can be made into a paste with the addition of water. Of these two options, the powdered form is better. However, there is no substitute for the real thing and if you get the chance, you owe it to yourself to try freshly grated wasabi root.

Pork Potstickers

Potsticker dumplings are a hands-down favorite in my cooking classes at Tsunami. I like to get the whole class involved. Many hands make short work. If you have the filling made and the wrappers on hand, all you need is a few willing participants and you'll soon have all the dumplings you can eat. The good thing about these dumplings is that they rarely make it to the dining room, so there are no dishes to clean up. Have a big platter and a lot of chopsticks nearby and throw a dumpling party in the kitchen.

1½ lb. green cabbage, finely chopped

1 tbsp. kosher salt

2½ lb. ground pork

1½ oz. ginger, minced

¾ cup chopped green onions

2 tbsp. soy sauce

2 tbsp. sesame oil

2 pkg. potsticker wrappers

2 tbsp. flour mixed with 2 tbsp. cold water to make a "slurry"

Peanut or vegetable oil

½ cup water

Shredded cabbage

Sprinkle the cabbage with the salt and allow to sit for 10-15 minutes in a colander. Strain and squeeze out the excess liquid. Mix the cabbage with the pork, ginger, onions, soy sauce, and sesame oil in a large bowl. Lay out 10-12 potsticker wrappers on a clean, dry work surface. Place about 2 tsp. filling in the center of each wrapper. Dab the edges of each wrapper with the slurry, and then fold over to form a half-moon shape. Seal well by pressing down with your fingers. The filling mixture freezes well. Use as much as you need at one time, and then seal the rest in a freezer bag. Squeeze all of the excess air out of the bag and flatten the filling out in the bag. That way, when you decide to make potstickers again, the filling will thaw quickly.

Preheat a large, flat-bottomed skillet. Add enough peanut or vegetable oil to just cover the bottom of the pan. Carefully place as many of the potstickers as you can fit into the pan without overcrowding. Cook until the dumplings begin to brown on the bottom, then add the water to the skillet and immediately cover with a tight-fitting lid. Steam the dumplings until they are translucent and the filling is firm. By this time all or nearly all of the water should have steamed away. Be careful that the pan doesn't dry out too quickly or you will scorch the dumplings.

When the dumplings are done, remove them with a metal spatula to a big platter lined with shredded cabbage. Have chopsticks and Chile-Soy Dipping Sauce (see index) at the ready, because these morsels are best eaten fresh out of the pan. Continue cooking and eating until all the dumplings are gone. **Makes about 50 dumplings.**

Shrimp Potstickers

1 lb. medium shrimp, peeled and deveined

2 tsp. chopped garlic

1 tbsp. chopped ginger

1 tsp. sesame oil

2 tbsp. mushroom-flavored soy sauce

2 green onions, sliced

2 tbsp. chopped water chestnuts (fresh ones, if possible)

1 pkg. potsticker wrappers

Place shrimp, garlic, ginger, sesame oil, and soy sauce into the bowl of a food processor and pulse until mixture is smooth. Remove from the food processor to a bowl and fold in the green onions and water chestnuts by hand. Refrigerate until ready to use. Any unused filling can be frozen in a tightly sealed freezer bag. Follow the preparation method in the Pork Potstickers recipe above. Serve with Chile-Soy Dipping Sauce (see index). **Makes about 25 dumplings.**

Scallop Potstickers

1 lb. sea scallops

1 tbsp. sake

¼ tsp. salt

1 tbsp. chopped ginger

2 green onions, sliced

1½ pkg. potsticker wrappers

Place scallops, sake, salt, and ginger into the bowl of a food processor and pulse until mixture is smooth. Remove from the food processor to a bowl and fold in the green onions by hand. Refrigerate until ready to use. Follow the preparation method in the Pork Potstickers recipe above. Serve with Sweet and Sour Sauce (see index). **Makes about 36 dumplings.**

Cold Sesame Noodles

This satisfying noodle dish originated in Japan, where the use of buckwheat, or soba, was popularized hundreds of years ago. Soba noodles have a chewy, almost crumbly texture to them. They are most enjoyable served cold, like in this recipe, with a simple dressing.

2 tbsp. sesame seeds

1 6-oz. pkg. buckwheat soba noodles

Boiling salted water

1 tbsp. chopped ginger

1 clove garlic, minced

4 tbsp. soy sauce

1 tbsp. sesame oil

1 bunch green onions, sliced

2 tbsp. olive oil

Toast the sesame seeds by placing them in a dry skillet and heating over medium heat until they begin to jump. Jiggle the pan so the seeds move around and toast evenly.

Cook the soba noodles in the water until al dente. Drain and cool. Toss in a bowl with the ginger, garlic, soy sauce, sesame oil, green onions, and olive oil. Mix until the noodles are well coated. Chill well before serving. Garnish with the toasted sesame seeds. **Serves 4.**

Thai Poppers

When I lived in San Francisco, my friends and I would often go to one of our favorite Thai restaurants on Geary. The menu was huge and we would always order by the number of the dish instead of trying to butcher the Thai pronunciation. The servers there were fantastic and had the entire menu memorized, so that when we called out our numbers, they knew exactly what dish we had ordered and would recite it to us. One dish that we always ordered was a hands-on appetizer that the entire table would share. I don't remember the name (or the number) of the dish, but I have spent years trying to recreate it. I call these Thai Poppers, because once you assemble them, you pop them into your mouth and eat them. They are highly addictive.

1 pkg. square won-ton wrappers

3 or 4 jalapeño peppers

1 medium root fresh ginger, peeled

1 bulb garlic, separated into cloves and peeled

½ lb. Chinese sausage, cooked

1 jar roasted, shelled peanuts

1 jar Chinese plum sauce

Cut the won-ton wrappers in half from one corner to another to form 2 triangles. Arrange the wrappers in a stack on a platter large enough to hold 6 small individual bowls. Dice the jalapeños, ginger, garlic, and Chinese sausage into cubes about the size of small peas. Place all of the diced ingredients into their respective, individual bowls. Put the peanuts and the plum sauce into their own bowls and arrange them on the platter.

Now the fun part: Take one of the won-ton wrappers and shape it into a cone. Fill it with one piece each of peanut, jalapeño, ginger, garlic, and Chinese sausage. Top the cone with a dab of plum sauce, then pop the whole thing in your mouth.

Most people trying this for the first time are a little skeptical about chewing up chunks of garlic, jalapeño, and ginger. But after one of these, you are hooked. After the first one or two poppers, you can begin experimenting with variations of ratios to suit your own tastes: a little more jalapeño, more ginger, no Chinese sausage, two peanuts. Everyone will begin to customize the poppers to their individual tastes. My favorite thing about this dish is that it is a real icebreaker at a party. At first you may have one or two folks putting together some poppers while a bunch of other people sort of watch from the fringe. Before long everyone wants to get in on the fun and you may find yourself cutting up more ginger, garlic, and jalapeños in the middle of your party.

Crab and Vegetable Spring Rolls
with Lemon-Chive Aioli

Spring rolls originated in China, where they were traditionally served to celebrate either the first day of spring or the sowing of the first crops of the new year. This uncooked version of spring roll exhibits a Vietnamese influence, since the wrapper is made of rice paper instead of the more traditional Chinese wrapper made from a flour-based dough. These are best served in the spring and summer when the vegetables are freshest.

Lemon-Chive Aioli

2 egg yolks

¼ tsp. salt

1 small clove garlic, minced

Juice of 1 lemon

½ cup olive oil

2 tbsp. chopped chives

Spring Rolls

1 yellow squash

1 zucchini

1 red bell pepper

1 bunch green onions

6 square sheets rice paper

½ lb. lump crabmeat, picked through for cartilage

To make the aioli, place the yolks into a stainless-steel bowl along with the salt, garlic, and lemon juice. Whisk until smooth. Slowly drizzle in the olive oil while whisking. Fold in the chives. The sauce should have the consistency of thin mayonnaise. Put the sauce in a squeeze bottle or a small baggie with one of the corners cut out.

Cut the yellow squash and zucchini into a fine julienne using a mandoline. Seed and julienne the red pepper. Cut off the white part of the green onions.

To assemble the spring rolls, have a large bowl of warm water on hand. Soak 1 sheet rice paper in the warm water until pliable. Lay the rice paper on a clean, dry towel with one of the corners facing you. Lay out a horizontal line of the vegetables stretching from one corner to the other. Squirt a generous line of the aioli on top of the vegetables, then top it with an ounce or so of crabmeat. Take the corner nearest you and fold it tightly over the filling. Then fold in either side and roll into a tight cylinder. Repeat with the remaining rice paper. Cut each roll into 3 or 4 pieces. **Serves 6.**

Fried Eggplant Stuffed with Shrimp and Chinese Sausage

2 eggplants, about 1 lb. each

1 recipe Shrimp Potstickers filling (see index)

4 oz. Chinese sausage, cooked and diced small

Flour

6 eggs, beaten

4 cups *panko* (Japanese breadcrumbs)

Peanut oil for frying

Peel the eggplants and slice them into ½-inch-thick rounds. Keep the slices in order after cutting them.

In a stainless-steel bowl, fold together the potsticker filling and the Chinese sausage. Spoon about 1 oz. filling on an eggplant slice. Top with the next slice of eggplant to make a sandwich. Mash down so that the filling reaches to the edges.

Set up a breading station by placing 3 pans side by side. (Cake pans with high sides are ideal.) Place the flour in one pan, the eggs in the second pan, and the *panko* in the third. Starting with the flour, coat several of the eggplant sandwiches and shake off the excess flour. (When breading, always keep one hand dry. In other words, don't dip in the eggs the same hand you used to flour something.) Dip the flour-coated eggplant sandwiches in the beaten eggs, then into the *panko*, using your dry hand to gently pack on the crumbs. Continue until all of the eggplant is breaded.

Preheat an electric wok half full of peanut oil to 350 degrees. Fry 3 or 4 of the eggplant sandwiches at a time until golden brown, turning once. Remove to a cookie sheet lined with absorbent paper and keep in a warm oven until ready to serve. **Makes about 20 pieces.**

soups

The soups in this chapter do not specify yields. I have always found that misleading. It is better to make a big batch of soup so that you have enough for people to have seconds or even thirds. Besides, soup is almost always better warmed up the next day.

Chilled Avocado Soup

Pumpkin Soup with Curried Apple Chutney

This is a great fall soup using two seasonal ingredients.

1 medium pie pumpkin or 2 small, enough for about 4 lb. pulp

1 medium yellow onion, peeled and diced

1 tbsp. vegetable oil

1 tbsp. Chinese five-spice powder

2 tsp. freshly grated nutmeg

½ cup chopped fresh sage

2 qt. vegetable stock

1 cup half-and-half

Salt and pepper to taste

Chopped chives

Curried Apple Chutney

1 small yellow onion, peeled and diced small

2 tsp. vegetable oil

4 Granny Smith apples, peeled, cored, and diced small

1 tbsp. Madras curry powder

1 bay leaf

½ cup rice vinegar

½ cup brown sugar

Peel and seed the pumpkins and cut into golf-ball-sized chunks. In a medium stockpot, sauté the onion in the oil until soft. Add the five-spice powder, nutmeg, and sage and stir for 30 seconds.

Add the pumpkin and stock. The liquid should just barely cover the pumpkin. Bring to a boil, stir, and reduce to a simmer. Cook until the pumpkin pieces can be easily mashed with the back of a spoon.

Cool soup slightly and puree in food processor while still warm. At this point the soup can be cooled down entirely and kept in the refrigerator for a day or reheated and served immediately. Add the half-and-half before reheating and season with salt and pepper while the soup is hot.

To make the chutney, sauté onion in oil until soft. Add the apples and curry powder and stir until the apples are well coated. Add the bay leaf, vinegar, and brown sugar. Bring to a boil, reduce to a simmer, and cook until the apples are tender but not falling apart. Garnish soup with a spoonful of chutney and some chives.

2 lb. ground pork

1 tbsp. soy sauce

1 tbsp. sesame oil

1 tbsp. salt

1 tsp. pepper

8 oz. water chestnuts, chopped

1 tbsp. chopped ginger

2 tbsp. cornstarch

1 egg

4 qt. chicken stock

Equal parts cornstarch and cold water mixed to make a "slurry"

Salt to taste

In a stainless-steel bowl, place the pork, soy sauce, sesame oil, salt, pepper, water chestnuts, ginger, cornstarch, and egg. Mix until all ingredients are thoroughly incorporated. Shape into meatballs about the size of a large marble.

Bring the chicken stock to a boil. Drizzle in the cornstarch slurry while stirring to slightly thicken the stock. Add the meatballs, reduce to a simmer, and cook for about 30 minutes or until meatballs are cooked through. Season with salt.

Egg Drop Soup

This is a quick, easy, and wholly satisfying soup that can be made in minutes: Chinese comfort food.

4 qt. chicken stock

Cornstarch slurry (equal parts cornstarch and cold water)

10 eggs

Salt and pepper to taste

½ bunch green onions, sliced

Bring the chicken stock to a boil. Whisk in enough cornstarch slurry to just barely thicken the stock.

Crack the eggs into a bowl and, using a fork, break all of the yolks so that they run into the whites. Reduce the chicken stock to a simmer. Pour the broken eggs into the hot stock in a slow, steady stream. Use a long-handled spoon or spatula to stir the stock in a figure-eight motion while doing so.

Bring the stock back to a full boil to make sure the eggs are congealed. Season with salt and pepper. Garnish with green onions just before serving.

Hot and Sour Soup

While some of the ingredients in this recipe may seem a bit obscure to the Western cook, they are readily available in Asian markets. There is no substitute for the lily buds and mushrooms. The former give the soup its distinct aroma and flavor, and the latter add a wonderful chewy texture. Your efforts in finding these ingredients and making this soup will be greatly rewarded when you serve it to appreciative friends and family.

3 qt. chicken stock

1½ lb. ground pork

2 cups sliced shiitake mushrooms, about 3 oz.

½ cup dried wood ear mushrooms, soaked for 1 hour in cold water, then cut into bite-size pieces

30 lily buds (see sidebar)

8 oz. bamboo shoots, cut into matchstick-size pieces

6 eggs, beaten

½ cup rice vinegar

4 tsp. hot bean paste

4 tbsp. soy sauce

3 tbsp. cornstarch dissolved in 6 tbsp. cold water

Salt to taste

1 block firm tofu, diced

1 bunch cilantro, chopped

Bring the stock to a boil. Add the ground pork, mushrooms, and lily buds. Reduce to a simmer and cook for 20 minutes.

Add bamboo shoots and return to a boil. Pour in the beaten eggs while stirring. Add vinegar, bean paste, and soy sauce. Season to taste. Return to a boil and add the cornstarch slurry while stirring. Add the tofu and cilantro just before serving.

Lily Buds and Wood Ear Mushrooms

Lily buds are the dried buds of the tiger lily. They are an integral ingredient in hot and sour soup and impart a distinct sweet/musky/herbal flavor and an unmistakable aroma. They can be found in Asian markets, usually near the dried-mushroom section.

Wood ear mushrooms, also known as tree ear mushrooms, can be found fresh or dried in Asian markets. The name stems from the fact that they resemble ears. These mushrooms have a chewy texture and are quite mild in flavor. Dried wood ear mushrooms should be reconstituted in cold water for 1 hour (or hot water for ½ hour) before being used in stir-fries or soups. A dried wood ear mushroom will swell up to at least quadruple its size, so they must be cut after they are rehydrated.

Black Bean Soup with Smoked Chile Cream

The Tsunami version of black bean soup gets a double whammy of smoky heat from chipotle chiles. Chipotle chili powder gives the soup a spicy backbone, while the chipotle-cream garnish adds a punch. For variety, try a dollop of Tomatillo Salsa in place of the cream (see index).

4 tbsp. chipotles in adobo

½ cup sour cream

½ cup milk or half-and-half

Juice of 1 lime

4 cups dried black beans

2 yellow onions, diced small

3 tbsp. olive oil

2 tbsp. chipotle chili powder

1 tbsp. ground cumin

6 qt. water

Salt to taste

Place the chipotles, sour cream, half-and-half, and lime juice in a blender and puree until smooth. Funnel into a squeeze bottle.

Pick through the beans and discard any stones, then rinse in cold water. In a large saucepan or stockpot, cook the onions in oil until they begin to soften. Add the chili powder and cumin and stir until the onions are well coated.

Add the beans and water. Bring to a boil, reduce to a simmer, and cook until beans are quite tender, about 1 hour and 15 minutes. Puree beans in their liquid until smooth. Thin down with additional water if necessary. Then season to taste. Garnish each bowl of soup with a drizzle of the chipotle cream.

Portuguese Bean Soup

In Hawaii, Portuguese bean soup is as ubiquitous as chicken noodle soup is on the mainland. Just like chicken noodle soup, there are numerous versions. I like this one because it is easy and relatively quick to make. Like most soups, this one gets better the longer it sits.

2 cups diced celery

2 cups peeled and diced carrots

3-4 large yellow onions, peeled and diced (about 4 cups)

1 tbsp. vegetable oil

2 cups tomato puree

4 cups cooked kidney beans (if using canned, drain and rinse)

3 large baking potatoes, peeled and diced

1 gal. water

1½ lb. linguiça sausage,* cooked and sliced

Salt and pepper to taste

1 bunch cilantro, coarsely chopped

Sauté the celery, carrots, and onions in oil for 3 minutes, stirring. Add the tomato puree and stir well. Add beans, potatoes, and water. Bring to a boil, reduce to a simmer, and cook until potatoes are tender. Add linguiça and cook until the sausage is heated through. Season to taste. Add the cilantro just before serving.

*Linguiça is a Portuguese sausage laced with garlic. It can be found in Latin markets or in the butcher department of most large-city supermarkets. In a bind, kielbasa sausage may be substituted, but only reluctantly. If using kielbasa, brown the slices separately in a skillet to develop the flavor a bit more.

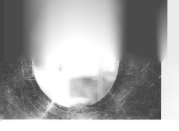

A quick, easy soup to make. It has just enough flavor from the mustard seed to caress the taste buds, but not enough to overpower the cauliflower. The Curry Oil adds a little heat to the first few spoonfuls.

2 heads cauliflower, about 3 lb.

1 medium yellow onion, diced

2 tbsp. butter or olive oil

8 cups water

1 tbsp. toasted, ground mustard seeds

1 qt. half-and-half

Kosher salt to taste

Cut the cauliflower into medium florets. In a large saucepan, cook the onions in butter or oil until soft. Add the cauliflower and water.

To toast the mustard seeds, heat in a dry skillet over medium heat until they begin to pop. (Have a lid close at hand, because the seeds will pop out of the pan.) Cover the pan immediately and remove from the heat. Keep the skillet covered until the seeds stop popping. Grind the mustard seeds in a spice grinder or with a mortar and pestle.

Add the ground mustard to the soup and cook, stirring occasionally, until the cauliflower is very tender. Puree the soup in a blender, and then return to the pan. Add the half-and-half and heat. Season with salt.

Curry Oil

4 tbsp. peanut or safflower oil

½ tsp. Madras curry powder

To make the Curry Oil, heat oil over low heat in a small saucepan until a drop of water sizzles when added. Remove from heat, add the curry powder, and cover. Allow the oil to sit until completely cool, then strain through a fine sieve lined with cheesecloth. Garnish each bowl of soup with a drizzle of Curry Oil. Curry Oil may be stored in a clean jar with a lid. This makes ¼ cup and will keep indefinitely.

Curried Butternut Squash Soup

I like this soup for its balance of sweetness and heat, which is enhanced by the buttery richness of the squash. You may serve this soup either hot or cold. If serving cold, you may want to fold in a bit of plain yogurt and adjust the salt accordingly.

5 lb. butternut squash

1 large yellow onion, peeled and sliced

2 tbsp. vegetable oil

2 tbsp. Madras curry powder

1 13.5-oz. can coconut milk

3 qt. water

Salt to taste

Peel the squash and scoop out the seeds. Dice the squash into golf-ball-sized chunks. Preheat a large stockpot and sauté the onions in the oil until soft.

Add the curry powder and stir until the onions are well coated. Add the coconut milk, bring to a boil, and then add the squash and water. Return to a boil, reduce to a simmer and cook until squash can be easily mashed with the back of a spoon. Season with salt and puree the soup in a blender while still warm.

Chilled Avocado Soup

This is a great soup for a first course before a grilled dinner. It's rather rich and substantial, so you should serve smaller portions if other food is to follow. But a large bowl with a dollop of picante salsa and a side of tortilla chips makes for a great lunch on a hot day.

8 ripe avocados

Juice of 1 lime

Juice of 1 lemon

2 cups plain, nonfat yogurt

2 cups low-fat milk

2 cups chilled vegetable stock

1 tsp. toasted, ground cumin seeds

½ medium red onion, diced small

Salt to taste

Peel and pit the avocados and toss them together in a large bowl with the lime juice, lemon juice, and yogurt. Puree the mixture in a food processor until smooth. Add the remaining ingredients and chill well before serving. You may thin the soup down with additional stock or milk.

Sweet Potato-Lemongrass Soup

This is a great soup for all seasons. It has a subtle heat on the finish from the peppers that is slightly muted by the rich sweetness of the potatoes and the coconut milk.

4 tbsp. unsalted butter

1 medium yellow onion, peeled and sliced

1 tbsp. minced ginger

5 large sweet potatoes, about 2½-3 lb., peeled and diced

4 stalks fresh lemongrass, white part only, minced

2 jalapeño peppers, seeded and minced

1 13.5-oz. can coconut milk

6 cups water

Salt to taste

In a heavy stockpot, melt the butter and add the onions. Sauté the onions until soft and add the ginger, sweet potatoes, lemongrass, and jalapeños. Cook for 5 minutes, stirring occasionally.

Add the coconut milk and water and bring to a boil. Reduce to a simmer and cook until potatoes are soft, about 40 minutes. Season with salt and puree the soup in a blender while still warm.

I have a friend who used to tell me, "Cilantro is God's way of getting you to eat soap." Okay, the guy was weird, but his point is that cilantro can have sort of a "soapy" flavor. Blanching the cilantro is a way to both preserve its bright green color and tone down its pungent taste. This soup is great as a palate cleanser or a first course before a light meal on a hot day.

2 bunches cilantro leaves

Boiling salted water

Ice water

Juice of 1 lime

1 jalapeño pepper, seeded and chopped

1 cup plain yogurt

½ cup sour cream

2 cups vegetable stock

½ tsp. toasted, ground cumin seeds

Salt and fresh ground black pepper to taste

Plunge the cilantro leaves in the boiling water for 10 seconds. Strain and immediately "shock" the cilantro in the ice water until cool. Place the cilantro in a blender along with the lime juice, jalapeño, yogurt, sour cream, stock, and cumin. Puree on high speed for 2 minutes. Stop the blender, scrape down the sides, then blend for 2 more minutes on high speed.

Season with salt and pepper. Chill thoroughly before serving.
Makes about 1 qt.

Cold Curried Eggplant Soup

This delicious chilled soup gets a little palate-warming heat courtesy of the Madras curry powder—a good example of yin and yang in a simple dish.

¼ cup unsalted butter

1 yellow onion, diced small

1 tbsp. Madras curry powder

1¼ lb. Chinese eggplant, peeled and cut into 2-inch slices

1 qt. vegetable stock

½ cup half-and-half

½ tsp. salt

¼ tsp. white pepper

Melt butter in medium saucepan. Add onion and cook until soft. Add curry powder and cook over low heat for 2 minutes.

Add eggplant and stock and bring to a boil. Reduce to a simmer and cook 30-40 minutes or until eggplant is soft. Puree soup in food processor while still warm. Add half-and-half, salt, and pepper. Chill overnight before serving.

Shrimp Gazpacho

This refreshingly cool soup originated in southern Spain. This version comes to America via Mexico. I prefer this chunky version to the pureed kind. Although gazpacho stands up fine on its own, I think the lightly poached shrimp give it a bit more substance for a well-rounded meal in a bowl. Other traditional and nontraditional garnishes include: small croutons tossed in melted butter and pan-toasted until crispy; diced, ripe avocado tossed in fresh lime juice; a dollop of crème fraiche or good-quality sour cream; chopped hard-boiled eggs.

1 lb. medium shrimp, shell on

1 clove garlic, minced

8 large, ripe tomatoes, peeled, seeded, diced small

1 large sweet onion (Vidalia, Maui, or Walla Walla), diced small

2 cucumbers, peeled, seeded, diced small

2 green bell peppers, seeded and minced

2 jalapeño peppers, seeded and minced

Juice of 2 lemons

Juice of 2 limes

½ cup chopped cilantro stems and leaves

1 46-oz. can tomato juice or V-8 juice

Salt and fresh-ground black pepper to taste

Bring a pan of salted water to a boil and add the shrimp. Poach the shrimp until just cooked, then peel, dice, and set aside. Combine the remaining ingredients in a large stainless-steel bowl and mix well. Serve in well-chilled bowls and garnish with a generous spoonful of the cooked shrimp and a sprig of fresh cilantro or your garnish of choice.

Oyster and Corn Chowder with Chipotle Croutons

I can't resist a good chowder. It's a meal in a bowl and almost a sin to not serve it with some sort of cracker or crusty bread. The chipotle croutons add both a crunch and a little smoky heat to this version.

1 stick unsalted butter

2 tbsp. chipotles in *adobo*, pureed

1 baguette, sliced into 1-inch-thick rounds

12 slices smoked bacon

4 cups diced yellow onion

2 cups diced celery

2 qt. clam juice

4 tbsp. chopped fresh thyme

6 cups fresh corn kernels

2 qt. half-and-half

6 potatoes, peeled and diced into thumbnail-sized cubes

4 dozen freshly shucked oysters

Salt and fresh-ground black pepper to taste

Mix the butter and chipotles. Butter each slice of baguette on one side with a generous amount of chipotle butter. Bake in a preheated 350-degree oven until crisp. Set aside.

Dice the bacon into small bits. (It is much easier to cut bacon while it is frozen.) Cook the bacon until crisp in a large pot. Drain the excess fat, but leave the bacon in the pot.

Add the onions and celery and cook for 1 minute, stirring. Add the clam juice, thyme, corn, and half-and-half. Bring to a boil, reduce to a simmer, and cook for 20 minutes, stirring occasionally. Add the potatoes and continue cooking until the potatoes are tender.

Add the shucked oysters, stir, and heat until they plump up. Season with salt and pepper. Serve immediately. Garnish each bowl with a chipotle crouton.

salads

These salads run the gamut from fresh greens dressed with a simple vinaigrette to a more elaborately composed affair that can be a meal in itself. The best salads are those that can be shared around the table with a group of friends and family.

Thai Beef Salad

Spinach Salad with Goat Cheese and Ginger-Soy Vinaigrette

The dressing on this salad is one of the most requested recipes by Tsunami patrons. It is a fabulous pairing with the spinach and goat cheese but has so many other applications. (With the addition of shiitake mushrooms it becomes the sauce for Mahi-Mahi with Shiitake Mushroom Vinaigrette.) While this dressing works great with delicate greens, it has enough backbone to stand up to a bitter green like arugula or curly endive.

¼ cup soy sauce

2 tsp. sugar

Juice of 1 lime

1 serrano pepper, minced

1 clove garlic, minced

½ cup rice vinegar

2 tsp. sesame oil

1 tbsp. chopped ginger

1 cup peanut oil

1 lb. fresh spinach

½ lb. goat cheese, crumbled

In a stainless-steel bowl, mix together the soy sauce, sugar, lime juice, serrano pepper, garlic, vinegar, sesame oil, and ginger. Whisk until the sugar dissolves. Slowly drizzle in the peanut oil while whisking.

Place the spinach in a large bowl, add enough vinaigrette to coat the leaves, and toss well. Plate on 6 chilled salad plates and top each serving with crumbled goat cheese. Serve immediately. **Serves 6.**

Chipotle Chicken Salad

I first made this on a whim for the staff meal (called "family meal" in the restaurant business) one day when I had some cooked chicken and extra chipotle aioli on hand. It has been a staff favorite ever since. I recently began offering it through my catering business, where it has elicited many requests for the recipe. Here it is.

5 lb. boneless, skinless chicken breasts

1 7-oz. can chipotles in adobo

2 cloves garlic, minced

Juice of 1 lime

1 tsp. salt

4 egg yolks

1 whole egg

1 cup olive oil

2 ribs celery, diced

3 green onions, sliced

Put the chicken in a pot and cover with cold water. Bring to a boil, reduce to a simmer, and gently cook the chicken until just done. Remove from the heat and allow to cool completely. Place the chipotles in a blender and puree until smooth. Add the garlic, lime juice, salt, egg yolks, and whole egg and puree until well blended. With the machine running, slowly drizzle in the olive oil until it is incorporated into the sauce. It should have the consistency of mayonnaise.

When the chicken is cool, dice and mix well with the chipotle aioli, celery, and green onions. Check for seasoning and add salt if necessary. Serve on your choice of bread as a sandwich or on a bed of greens. This is also great as an hors d'oeuvre served on individual tortilla chips. **Serves 10 to 12.**

Green Salad with Herb Vinaigrette and Blue Cheese

I love this simple vinaigrette made of fresh herbs, especially with a good blue cheese. Try the vinaigrette as a marinade for thinly shredded raw vegetables as well.

¼ cup fresh basil leaves, packed

¼ cup cilantro, stems and all

½ tsp. salt

½ tsp. sugar

Juice of 1 lemon

⅓ cup rice vinegar

⅔ cup olive oil

3 heads Boston or Bibb lettuce, rinsed and drained

6 oz. good-quality blue-veined cheese

Place the basil, cilantro, salt, sugar, lemon juice, and vinegar in blender and puree until smooth. With the machine running, slowly drizzle in the olive oil. Toss the lettuce with a generous amount of dressing in a large bowl until well coated. Arrange the leaves on 6 chilled salad plates, sprinkle each salad with blue cheese, and serve immediately. Any surplus dressing will keep in the refrigerator for up to 3 days. **Serves 6.**

Green Papaya Salad

I like to serve this as a side dish any time I do a family-style meal. This crisp, sometimes-fiery dish goes great with grilled seafood. The amount of chile pepper can be adjusted to increase the heat as much as you can stand it.

1 large green papaya

1 carrot, peeled

2 tsp. sugar

1 tsp. fish sauce

1 tbsp. rice vinegar

1 tbsp. mushroom-flavored soy sauce

½ small red onion, peeled and sliced thin

2 tbsp. chopped cilantro, stems and leaves

1 serrano pepper, seeded and chopped

Peel the papaya and cut in half lengthwise. Scoop out the seeds with a spoon. (The seeds should be white. As the papaya ripens, the seeds will turn darker until they are a greenish-black, at which time the papaya is fully ripe.) Shred the papaya and carrot on a mandoline with the fine-blade attachment. If you don't have a mandoline, you may use an old-fashioned box grater or a food processor with the grater-disk attachment.

Put the sugar in a stainless-steel bowl along with the fish sauce, vinegar, and soy sauce. Stir until the sugar dissolves. Add the papaya, carrot, onion, cilantro, and pepper. Toss all ingredients together well and let sit for at least ½ hour before serving. **Serves 6 as a side dish.**

Asian Chicken Salad with Sesame Dressing

I like this recipe even more than the Chipotle Chicken Salad. But both are nice alternatives to the deli-style chicken salad most people are familiar with.

2 whole fryer chickens (3½-4 lb. each) or about 3 lb. cooked chicken meat

½ cup soy sauce

½ cup rice vinegar

2 tbsp. sesame oil

3 tbsp. chopped ginger

4 tbsp. Dragon Juice (see index)

¾ cup peanut oil

1 bunch green onions, green part only, sliced

Put the chickens in a pot and cover with cold water. Bring to a boil, reduce to a simmer, and cook for 30-35 minutes or until cooked through. Remove the chickens and let them cool slightly. Pick the meat and skin off the chickens. (You may return all the bones and other scraps to the cooking liquid, add 2 diced onions, 1 carrot, and 2 celery ribs, and simmer for another 45 minutes to make a chicken stock.)

Shred the chicken meat into long strips by hand. In a stainless-steel bowl, mix the chicken meat well with the remaining ingredients. Serve on a bed of mixed greens, in a sandwich, or on top of crisp-fried won-ton wrappers as an hors d'oeuvre. **Serves 6 to 12.**

Thai Beef Salad

This is one of my favorite summertime salads. It hits all the right flavor notes for me. The spicy, sweet, citric tang of the dressing is the perfect foil for the charred flavor of the grilled beef. Serve it as an entrée, or make a heaping platter to share with a group of people. An ice-cold beer is the obvious beverage choice for this dish.

Dressing

¼ cup cilantro, stems and leaves, coarsely chopped

2 jalapeño peppers, chopped, seeds and all

2 cloves garlic, minced

1 tbsp. dark brown sugar

2 tbsp. fish sauce

½ tsp. pepper

½ cup fresh-squeezed lemon juice

1 tbsp. chopped fresh lemongrass

Salad

1 lb. flank steak

Salt and fresh-ground black pepper

1 small red onion, peeled and sliced thin

1 ripe tomato, diced

2 cucumbers, peeled and sliced thin

½ cup chopped fresh mint

1 head romaine lettuce, rinsed

Prepare a charcoal grill. Once the flames subside, bank the coals to one side of the grill so that there is a hot side and a "cool" side. Place all the ingredients for the dressing in a blender and blend until smooth.

Season the steak with salt and pepper. Put the steak on a medium-hot grill and cook 6-8 minutes on one side, then grill the other side for the same amount of time. Move the steak over to the cool side of the grill and put a lid on it while you prepare the rest of the salad.

In a large stainless-steel bowl, place the onion, tomato, cucumbers, and mint. Toss until well mixed. Reserve 4 large leaves of romaine to serve as the base of the salad. Tear the rest of the leaves into big pieces and toss in the bowl with the other ingredients.

Remove the steak from the grill and allow it to "rest" for about 5 minutes on a cutting board. With a sharp, long-bladed knife, slice the steak across the grain into thin strips. Toss the steak in the bowl with the lettuce, tomatoes, cucumbers, onions, and mint. Be sure to add the drippings from the cutting board, as that is an integral part of the salad. Add the dressing, toss well, and serve on plates lined with the whole romaine leaves. **Serves 4.**

Spicy Shrimp Salad

This is a shrimp variation on the Thai Beef Salad.

Dressing

½ cup cilantro, stems and leaves, chopped

2 jalapeño peppers, minced

2 cloves garlic, minced

2 tbsp. fish sauce

½ cup fresh-squeezed lemon juice

Salad

2 lb. medium shrimp, peeled and deveined

2 tbsp. chopped fresh lemongrass

1 tsp. pepper

2 tsp. kosher salt

2 tsp. peanut oil

1 red onion, sliced thin

1 pt. small, sweet tomatoes like Mexican Midgets, Sweet 100s, or Teardrop, halved

1 small cucumber, peeled and sliced into thin rounds

½ cup fresh mint, chopped

2 heads Boston or Bibb lettuce, rinsed and drained

Place all the dressing ingredients in a blender and puree until smooth. In a stainless-steel bowl, toss together the shrimp, lemongrass, pepper, and salt. Preheat a sauté pan until it is smoking hot. Add the oil and then the shrimp. Cook until the shrimp begin to turn pink, then turn them over and cook until done.

Remove the shrimp to a clean stainless-steel bowl; add the dressing, onion, tomatoes, cucumbers, and mint. Portion equally on 6 plates lined with the lettuce. **Serves 6.**

Crab and Celery Root Salad with Lemon-Chive Aioli

Celery root, or celeriac, as it is also known, is the root of a particular celery that is cultivated just for its root. It has a wonderful celery-herb flavor, which I find is a greatly enhanced by the lemon and chive aioli in this recipe. Celery root, will oxidize so dress it soon after you peel it.

4 egg yolks
1 whole egg
1 clove garlic, minced
Juice of 2 lemons
1 cup olive oil
2 tbsp. chopped chives
2 lb. peeled celery root
Kosher salt to taste
12 oz. jumbo lump crabmeat

Place the egg yolks, whole egg, garlic, and lemon juice in a blender and blend until smooth. With the machine running, slowly drizzle in the olive oil. Remove to a stainless-steel bowl and stir in the chives until well mixed.

Grate the celery root using the grating attachment on a food processor or by hand on a box grater. Fold the grated celery root into the dressing until well coated. Season with salt.

Divide salad equally onto 6 chilled plates. Top each portion with 2 oz. crabmeat. **Serves 6.**

fish

Fish is my favorite medium to work with in the kitchen. I love the many different characteristics that are unique to each species of fish. Discovering the best method of cooking and presenting each piece of fish we cut at Tsunami is a challenge that never gets old.

Grilled Salmon with Chipotle Corn Pudding and Tomatillo Salsa

Fish consumption has increased dramatically over the past ten years. Not only are people eating more fresh fish, they are eating a greater variety of fish. With increased consumption has come an increase in fish cookery at home. I have hosted a lot of fish-cooking classes over the years at the restaurant. The thing that always strikes me is most people's complete puzzlement when it comes to cooking fish. One of the most popular classes is the "Hawaiian Mystery Box" class. I have a box full of fish shipped overnight from a fish company in Honolulu. (I have been dealing with this company for years, so they know how my tastes run and I trust them to send me only the best of what is coming off the boats, no matter what it is. I never know what I am getting until I open the box.)

The students in the class love the anticipation of opening up the box to see what is inside just as much as I do. Most of my students have never seen a whole fillet of opah (moonfish), or a ruby red tombo (albacore tuna), or Pele snapper, nairagi, kajiki, ono, or hebi. Initially the class is a bit overwhelmed by the variety of textures and colors of these fabulous fish samples. But as I go over the different qualities, and textures, and flavor profiles of each fish, then explain the different cooking techniques that apply to the different styles of fish, things begin to make sense.

Cooking fish should not be a mystery; it should be an adventure. Most fish is inexpensive enough that you can afford to learn by trial and error. These recipes will help give you some idea of the myriad cooking techniques for fish. I encourage you to experiment on your own, once you have gained a level of self-confidence. Fish should not be feared. One of the most important things to remember (apart from freshness) is to not overcook fish. No matter where you live or where you shop, you should get to know your fishmonger. Shop in a reputable market that has a high rate of turnover on seafood. That way, at least you know that fish is not hanging around for a long time. Don't be afraid to ask the sales clerk to let you smell the fish. Fresh fish should not smell like fresh fish. It should have a clean, oceanlike aroma, slightly reminiscent of cucumber.

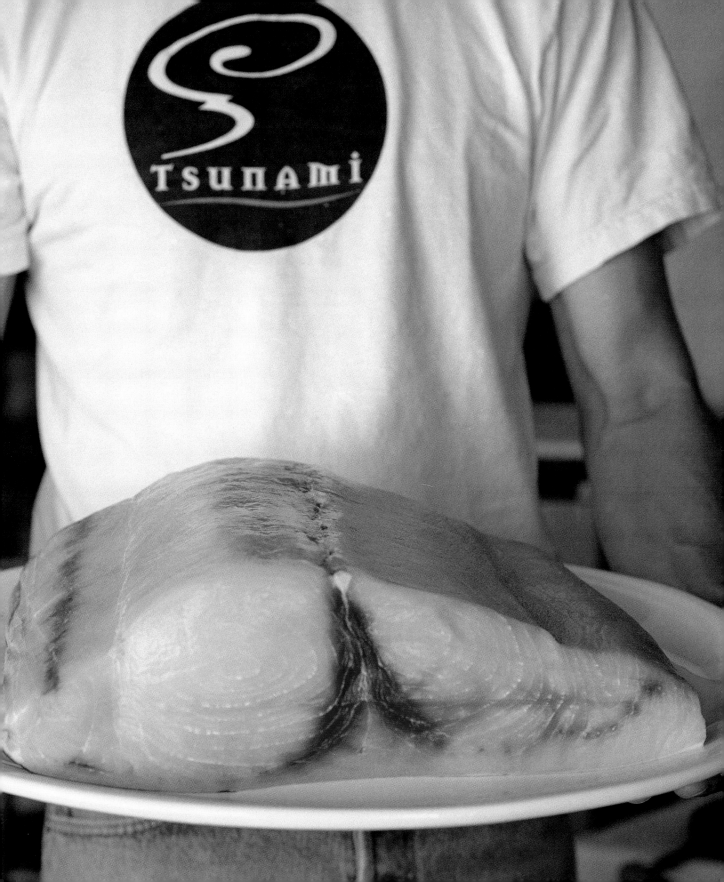

Sautéed Mahi-Mahi with Grilled Shrimp Salsa

Juice of 1 lime

Juice of 1 tangerine or orange

1 jalapeño pepper, seeded and chopped

2 cloves garlic, minced

¼ olive oil

1 lb. medium shrimp, shell on

2 tbsp. chopped cilantro

1 tbsp. toasted, ground coriander seed

1 tbsp. olive oil

Salt and fresh-ground black pepper to taste

6 fillets mahi-mahi, 6-7 oz. each

Kosher salt

2 tbsp. olive oil

Mix together the lime juice, tangerine or orange juice, jalapeño, garlic, and ¼ cup oil in a stainless-steel or glass bowl. Place the shrimp in the marinade, stir until well coated, and allow to marinate for 30 minutes. Prepare a charcoal grill or preheat a grill plate on top of the stove. Remove the shrimp from the marinade and allow them to drain in a colander set inside a bowl. Discard the marinade.

Place the shrimp on a hot grill and cook until pink, then remove them to a clean bowl and let them cool to room temperature. Peel and chop the shrimp coarsely and add the cilantro, coriander, and 1 tbsp. oil. Salt and pepper to taste.

Season the mahi-mahi fillets on one side with kosher salt. Add the oil to a hot skillet and place the fish in, salted side down. Cook until golden brown, then turn over and continue to cook until cooked through. Serve the mahi-mahi with a big scoop of the shrimp salsa. **Serves 6.**

Vinaigrette as a Sauce for Fish

I have found that a light, citrus-based vinaigrette is a great alternative to a heavier sauce, especially with grilled seafood. Citrus and seafood have a natural affinity for one another anyway. And the healthy aspects of a vinaigrette with grilled fish cannot be ignored either.

Experiment with different combinations of citrus juices: blood orange, grapefruit, key lime, kumquat, and tangerine. Add a little sugar to cut the acidity when using sharper-flavored citrus. Using a mild vinegar in conjunction with citrus juices can result in a good balance of sweet and savory acidity. See the "Basic Recipes and Side Dishes" chapter for other citrus vinaigrette recipes.

Seared Tuna with Citrus-Crab Vinaigrette

2 tbsp. fresh-squeezed lime juice

2 tbsp. fresh-squeezed lemon juice

¾ cup fresh-squeezed orange juice

1 large shallot, minced

1 clove garlic, minced

2 tsp. chopped fresh thyme

2 tsp. chopped fresh parsley

½ tsp. salt

1 cup olive oil

6 yellowfin tuna steaks, about 1½ inches thick

Kosher salt

2 tbsp. olive oil

1 lb. jumbo lump crabmeat

Place the citrus juices, shallot, garlic, thyme, parsley, and salt in a stainless-steel bowl. Slowly drizzle in the 1 cup oil while whisking. Set the vinaigrette aside until ready to serve.

Season the tuna steaks on one side with a sprinkle of kosher salt. Preheat a sauté pan or cast-iron skillet, add the oil, and add the tuna steaks, salted side down. Cook just long enough for the fish to start to brown. Turn over and cook for a couple of minutes more. You can judge the doneness of the fish by looking at the sides. Leave a good margin of red on the sides of the fish for rare. The less you cook tuna, the better it is. The contrast between a good, seared surface and a tender, cool, melt-in-the-mouth center is out of this world.

To serve, ladle about 2 oz. vinaigrette on each of 6 plates, stirring the vinaigrette each time. Sprinkle about 2½ oz. crabmeat on each plate and spread it around evenly. Top with the seared tuna and serve immediately. **Serves 6.**

Grilled Swordfish with Avocado-Orange Salad and Citrus-Chile Vinaigrette

2 oranges, peeled and segmented

2 tbsp. chopped cilantro

Juice of 1 lemon

Juice of 1 lime

3 green onions, green part only, sliced

2 ripe avocados (but rather firm)

Kosher salt to taste

4 swordfish steaks, 6-8 oz. each

Pepper to taste

Cooked rice

Vinaigrette

Juice of 1 lime

Juice of 1 lemon

Juice of 1 orange

1 jalapeño pepper, minced

1 clove garlic, minced

2 tsp. Thai fish sauce

1 tsp. kosher salt

½ cup olive oil

Prepare a charcoal grill. While the coals are getting hot, prepare the salad. Place the orange segments, cilantro, lemon juice, lime juice, and green onions in a stainless-steel or glass bowl. Peel and dice the avocados into nice big chunks and toss them in the bowl. Gently mix the ingredients together with your fingers. Salt to taste and set aside.

Place all vinaigrette ingredients except for the oil in a stainless-steel or glass bowl. Slowly drizzle in the oil while whisking.

Before placing the swordfish on the grill, make sure the coals are white hot and the grill is clean. Wipe the grill grids with a grill towel lightly dipped in oil. Season the swordfish steaks on one side with salt and pepper and place them, seasoned side down, on the grill. I think swordfish is best when cooked to medium. Don't bog yourself down with trying to time something on the grill. It never works. Cook the swordfish until it is done and not a second longer. It's as simple as that.

Remove the swordfish from the grill and plate it immediately. Plop a big spoonful of the avocado-orange salad on one end of the fish and ladle a couple of ounces of the vinaigrette on top of the salad. Serve with a scoop of plain rice to soak up all the juices. **Serves 4.**

Sautéed Snapper with Celery-Root Salad and Citrus Vinaigrette

When grated, celery root will turn brown, like a raw potato, so it is important to use an acidic element when serving it raw.

1 bulb celery root

3 egg yolks

Juice of 1 lemon

2 cloves garlic, minced

½ tsp. salt

1 cup olive oil

Salt to taste

6 fillets snapper, 6-7 oz. each

Kosher salt

1 tbsp. olive oil

1 recipe Citrus Vinaigrette (see index)

25-30 orange segments for garnish

Peel the celery root and rinse well in cold water. Grate the celery root and set aside. Place egg yolks in bowl of an electric mixer along with the lemon juice, garlic, and ½ tsp. salt. Run mixer for 30 seconds. With the machine running, slowly drizzle in the 1 cup oil until the sauce has the consistency of mayonnaise. Remove from the machine and fold into the grated celery root. Mix well and adjust the seasoning with salt to taste.

Dab the snapper fillets dry with a paper towel and season them on one side with a sprinkle of kosher salt. Heat a large sauté pan and add the oil. Gently place the fish in the pan, salted side down, and cook until golden brown. Turn the fillets and continue cooking until fish is cooked through.

Serve a spoonful of the celery-root salad on each of 6 plates. Ladle 2 oz. vinaigrette around the salad and top with the snapper. Garnish each plate with 4 or 5 orange segments. **Serves 6.**

Seared Tuna with Stir-Fried Bok Choy and Sambal Aioli

We seemed to have a surplus of tuna one night at the restaurant, so I challenged my sous-chef to prepare a special that would help us sell some of it. He presented me with this simple dish. I liked it so much that I ate it for dinner for the next three nights. This plate has a lot of the elements that I like to see in a menu item. First of all it is simple. Secondly it is a clean, unfussed-with presentation. And lastly, but most importantly, it has a variety of textures, flavors, and colors. To me, this dish approaches the sublime.

2 egg yolks

¼ tsp. salt

Juice of 1 lime

2 tsp. sambal

¾ cup olive oil

2 lb. bok choy, rinsed

2 tbsp. peanut oil

½ cup vegetable stock

½ cup Chile-Soy Dipping Sauce (see index)

2 tsp. cornstarch dissolved in 1 tbsp. vegetable stock

6 fillets yellowfin tuna, 6-7 oz. each

Kosher salt

2 tbsp. olive or peanut oil

To make the aioli, place the egg yolks, ¼ tsp. salt, lime juice, and sambal in a blender and blend until smooth. With the machine running, slowly drizzle in the olive oil. The sauce should have the consistency of mayonnaise.

Rinse the bok choy and cut the white stalks at an angle about 1 inch wide. Cut or tear the green leaves into big pieces. Preheat a wok or a large sauté pan. Add 2 tbsp. peanut oil and heat. Add the bok choy and cook, stirring frequently, until the greens are wilted and the white of the bok choy begins to soften slightly. Add the vegetable stock and the chile-soy sauce. Bring the liquid to a boil. Cook for 1 minute, stirring. Stir the cornstarch mixture and pour it into the bok choy, stirring well.

While the bok choy is cooking, season the tuna fillets with a little kosher salt. Place them into a large preheated sauté pan to which has been added 2 tbsp. olive or peanut oil. Cook on high heat for about 2 minutes, and then turn the fillets over. Cook them for an additional 2 minutes.

Stir the bok choy well and with a pair of tongs, place a big pile on each of 6 warm plates. When all the bok choy is portioned, evenly drizzle whatever sauce remains in the pan onto each plate. Place 1 fillet of tuna on top of each pile of bok choy. Spoon a generous dollop of the sambal aioli on top of each fish and serve immediately. **Serves 6.**

Sambal

In Indonesia, sambal *refers to a wide range of side dishes and condiments. Any mention of* sambal *in this book refers to* sambal ulek, *which is a mixture of fresh hot chiles that has been ground with salt, vinegar, and sometimes garlic, and bottled. I use it like some people use ketchup. Sambal is available in Asian markets and some grocery stores.*

Cornmeal-Crusted Grouper with Gazpacho Vinaigrette

Obviously, I can't get enough of vinaigrettes with fish. This flaky fish with a crusty outside goes great with the crisp vegetables in the gazpacho.

Vinaigrette

1 clove garlic, minced

1 large, ripe tomato, diced small

½ sweet onion (Vidalia, Maui, or Walla Walla), diced small

1 cucumber, peeled, seeded, and diced small

½ green bell pepper, diced small

1 jalapeño pepper, minced

Juice of 1 lemon

2 tbsp. champagne vinegar

½ cup olive oil

4 tbsp. chopped cilantro

Salt and fresh-cracked black pepper to taste

Fish

6 fillets grouper, 6-8 oz. each

Kosher salt

½ cup cornmeal

1 tbsp. olive oil

Mix all the vinaigrette ingredients together well. Take 1 cup of the mixture and puree in a blender until smooth. Add back to the remaining vinaigrette and keep chilled until ready to use.

Dab the grouper fillets dry with a paper towel and season with kosher salt. Dredge the fillets in the cornmeal on one side. Place them, cornmeal side down, in a hot sauté pan with the oil. Cook until the cornmeal turns crisp, then turn the fillets over and continue cooking until done through. To serve, ladle the gazpacho vinaigrette onto each of 6 plates, top with the grouper, and serve immediately. **Serves 6.**

Ginger-Steamed Snapper with Black Bean Sauce

Steamed fish with black bean sauce is a classic Chinese combination. Infusing the fish with fresh ginger adds an element that plays well off the black bean sauce.

3 cloves garlic, minced

1 tbsp. chopped ginger

1 tbsp. peanut oil

2 tsp. sambal

2 tbsp. mushroom-flavored soy sauce

2 tbsp. Chinese black beans, coarsely chopped

4 green onions, sliced

2 cups vegetable stock

1 tsp. sesame oil

1 tbsp. cornstarch dissolved in 1 tbsp. water or vegetable stock

6 fillets snapper, 6-7 oz. each

6 tbsp. minced ginger

6 green onions, green part only, sliced

Preheat a small saucepan and briefly cook the garlic and ginger in the peanut oil. Add the sambal, soy sauce, black beans, and green onions. Stir 3 or 4 times then add the vegetable stock. Bring to a boil, reduce to a simmer, and cook for 5 minutes. Add the sesame oil, then, with the sauce boiling, stir in the cornstarch mixture just until the sauce thickens slightly.

You can rig up a steamer by placing a wire rack inside of a large roasting pan. Add 2 inches water to the pan and bring to a boil. Place the snapper fillets on a heatproof platter. Evenly portion the 6 tbsp. ginger on top of the snapper fillets. Top with the sliced green onions and place the platter on the wire rack in the steamer. Cover the pan tightly with aluminum foil and steam for about 8 minutes or until the snapper is flaky. Gently remove snapper with a slotted metal spatula. Serve on warm plates with the black bean sauce ladled on top. **Serves 6.**

Chinese Black Beans

Unlike the dried black beans popular in Latin American cooking, these are soybeans that have been fermented and salted as a form of preservation. Although strong tasting on their own, they impart a delicate flavor when cooked.

Grilled Salmon with Chipotle Corn Pudding and Tomatillo Salsa

4 cups fresh corn kernels

Boiling salted water

3 oz. unsalted butter

½ cup sugar

4 eggs

1 7-oz. can chipotles in *adobo*, pureed

1 tsp. salt

2½ cups whole milk

8 fillets wild salmon, 6-8 oz. each

Kosher salt

1 recipe Tomatillo Salsa (see index)

Cook the corn kernels in the water until tender. Drain and cool. Place the butter and sugar in the bowl of an electric mixer. With the paddle attachment, whip until butter is fluffy. Scrape the sides and bottom of the bowl. Add the eggs, one at a time, mixing until incorporated before adding another. Add the chipotle puree and whip on low speed until well blended. Add the salt and the corn kernels. With the machine running, slowly add the milk and continue mixing. Pour the mixture into 8 8-oz. ovenproof ramekins that have been generously buttered. Place the ramekins on a baking sheet in a 400-degree oven, uncovered, and bake for 45 minutes to 1 hour or until set in the center.

Pat the salmon fillets dry with a paper towel and season on one side with a sprinkle of kosher salt. Place them on a medium-hot grill, salted side down, and grill to medium doneness, turning once. Serve immediately with a ramekin of Chipotle Corn Pudding and a dollop of Tomatillo Salsa draped over the fish. **Serves 8.**

Sesame Fried Snapper with Asian Slaw

I have fond memories of outdoor fish fries down at my grandpa's house whenever my mother's side of the family all got together. Grandpa would set up the electric skillet as far out into the yard as all the extension cords would allow him (just so we wouldn't set the house on fire when one of the kids knocked over the hot grease). Uncle Lowell would show up with more catfish than you think a group of people could ever eat. Grandma would bring out a big bucket of hushpuppy batter and before long the air was filled with the scent of cornmeal-crusted catfish frying in hot oil.

As a kid I thought there was nothing better than a hot piece of catfish surreptitiously snatched off of the grease-splotched shopping bag on which it drained. Then I went to Australia and experienced a true version of fish and chips wrapped in newspaper. As I sat there eating a big slab of barramundi in crispy batter doused with malt vinegar, I thought to myself, "This comes close."

Both of those food memories are years ago and miles away. But this dish always makes me smile and think back to those outdoor summer fish fries.

Peanut oil for frying
1 cup all-purpose flour
1 tsp. baking powder
1 tbsp. cornstarch
2 tsp. salt
1¼ cups ice-cold water
½ cup sesame seeds
6 fillets skin-on snapper, about 6 oz. each
Additional flour for dredging
1 recipe Asian Slaw (see index)

Preheat the peanut oil to 350 degrees in an electric wok or a heavy saucepan. The oil should be at least 3 inches deep. In a large stainless-steel bowl, sift together 1 cup flour with the baking powder, cornstarch, and salt. Add the water and stir to break up the lumps of flour. Stir the sesame seeds into the batter. Keep batter cold until ready to use.

Dredge the snapper fillets in the flour and shake off the excess. Dip 1 piece of fish in the batter, wiping off the drips on the edge of the bowl. Carefully lower the fish into the hot oil about halfway. Once the fish begins to float, lower the rest of the fish into the oil, carefully. Repeat with remaining fillets. Cook until the fillets are golden brown and flaky on the inside. You may have to break one open to make sure it is done. Don't worry about it; even professional chefs do that. Remove fillets with a slotted spoon or a pair of tongs and drain on absorbent paper before serving. Serve each fillet with a generous heap of Asian Slaw. **Serves 6.**

Roasted Sea Bass on Black Thai Rice with Soy Beurre Blanc

This is by far our most popular menu item. In our first-ever review, a local restaurant critic called the sea bass "the entree that may soon become legendary." It has. When I first changed the menu back in 1999, I took the sea bass off because I felt as though my customers were not giving the other offerings a fair shake. Boy, was that a mistake! I got phone calls from people every day about the sea bass. I had people call me out to their tables to scold me for not having the sea bass. I had people walk out of the restaurant because we didn't have the sea bass. I had people tell me they would never come back to Tsunami until I brought the sea bass back. I had people beg, plead, threaten, and bribe me to bring the sea bass back. Finally, after a year of this nonsense (I'm a stubborn old coot), I gave in and brought the sea bass back. The good part of all this is that my "hardcore" regulars continued to frequent Tsunami and they actually tried the other entrees. Now my menu sales are a lot more balanced. I do still get phone calls from folks asking, "Y'all still got the sea bass, don't ya?" I do.

2 cups raw black Thai rice

4 cups cold water

2 tbsp. kosher salt

1 stalk fresh lemongrass, smashed

¼ cup sake or semidry white wine

1 tbsp. chopped ginger

¼ cup heavy whipping cream

½ lb. unsalted butter, cut into tbsp.-sized chunks

¼ cup good-quality soy sauce

4 fillets Chilean sea bass, 6-8 oz. each

Kosher salt

Olive oil

Place rice in a medium saucepan or stockpot with a thick bottom. Cover with some water and swish the rice around with your hand. Pour off the water and repeat the process several times until the water begins to run almost clear. Cover the rice with the 4 cups cold water and add the 2 tbsp. salt and lemongrass. Bring the rice to a boil on the stovetop, reduce to a simmer, and cook, covered, on very low heat for 35-40 minutes or until all the water has been absorbed. Remove the lemongrass stalk. Keep the rice covered until ready to serve.

To make the sauce, put the sake (or white wine) and ginger in a small saucepan. Bring to a boil, reduce to a simmer, and let cook until almost, but not quite, evaporated. Add the cream, bring to a boil, and allow to simmer until the cream begins to thicken. With the cream still on the heat, begin adding the chunks of butter to the saucepan while whisking. Whisk continuously, allowing each piece of butter to fully incorporate before adding the next piece. Whisk in the soy sauce. Set the beurre blanc aside in a warm, not hot, place until ready to serve.

Pat the sea bass fillets dry with a paper towel. Season each portion on one side with a little kosher salt. Preheat a heavy, thick-bottomed sauté pan on the stove, add a drizzle of olive oil, and then gently place the sea bass, salted side down, in the pan. Do not shake the pan or attempt to move the fish; just let it sit and cook for 5-6 minutes. Without turning the fish, place the entire pan in a preheated 400-degree oven.

While the fish finishes cooking in the oven (it will need another 5-6 minutes) begin your plate up. Use an ice-cream scoop with a thumb-action lever (trust me, this rice is so sticky you need help getting it off the scoop) to place a dollop of rice on the center of each plate. Ladle 2 or 3 oz. sauce around the rice.

Remove the sea bass from the oven and gently flip it over with a metal spatula. The top should be a nice golden brown. Test for doneness with a metal skewer. If there is any resistance, throw the fish back in the oven for a few more minutes. Place a portion of sea bass on top of each scoop of rice and serve immediately. **Serves 4.**

Spice-Crusted Tuna on Cucumber Salad
with Wasabi Vinaigrette

After the Roasted Sea Bass on Black Thai Rice, this is probably Tsunami's most popular dish. I don't dare take it off the menu, lest I suffer the wrath of our regular customers.

½ cup wasabi powder

½ cup water

1 clove garlic, minced

1 tbsp. chopped ginger

¼ cup rice vinegar

¼ cup soy sauce

2 tbsp. sesame oil

1 tsp. salt

2 cups peanut oil

4 tbsp. whole coriander

½ tsp. ground cinnamon

1 pod star anise

2 tbsp. Chinese five-spice powder

2 tsp. whole mustard seed

2 tsp. chili powder

4 cucumbers, peeled

8 yellowfin tuna steaks, 6-8 oz. each

Kosher salt

Olive oil

In a small bowl, mix together the wasabi powder and water until smooth. Invert the bowl on a plate and allow the paste to develop its flavor for about 5 minutes. Scrape the wasabi paste into a stainless-steel bowl. Add the garlic, ginger, vinegar, soy sauce, sesame oil, and salt and whisk until smooth. Slowly drizzle in the peanut oil while whisking. Set the vinaigrette aside until ready to serve.

Mix all the spices together. Grind them to a fine powder using a coffee grinder or a mortar and pestle. Sift through a fine sieve to remove the coriander husks.

Using a mandoline, cut the cucumbers into long, paper-thin ribbons. If you don't have a mandoline, a vegetable peeler will give you almost the same effect. Continue to slice each cucumber lengthwise until you reach the seeds, then turn the cucumber and slice again.

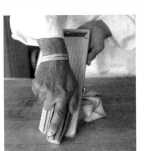

Season the tuna fillets with a little kosher salt then dredge them in the spice mix. Place the tuna into a preheated sauté pan or skillet with a little olive oil and cook 2 minutes on medium-high heat. Turn the fish over and cook for another 2 minutes.

To serve, toss the cucumber ribbons in a large bowl. Pour half of the vinaigrette on top and toss until well coated. With a ladle, drizzle the remainder of the vinaigrette onto each of 8 plates. Arrange a pile of cucumber salad on each plate, and then top with a portion of tuna. **Serves 8.**

Sautéed Mahi-Mahi with Grilled-Pineapple Salsa and Cilantro Pesto

I first came across grilled pineapple when I worked on a horse ranch just outside the small town of Sofala, New South Wales when I was traveling in Australia. Every Sunday afternoon there was a big cookout and along with their rissoles and dampers (meat patties and rustic bread), everyone got a big slab of grilled pineapple. I found the charred, sweet acidity to be a great foil for other foods, so I began making a salsa out of grilled pineapple.

The cilantro pesto was a result of a sort of "variation-on-a-theme" experiment, where I tried to make pesto out of every herb *but* basil. (With the exception of cilantro and sage, the results were predictably underwhelming. Rosemary pesto was a particularly bad idea.)

"Family meal" sometimes sparks the idea for a new special for next week's menu. Since family meal at Tsunami often consists of all the bits and bites of food that accumulate over the course of a couple of days, these repasts often bring together the oddest pairings of food. This is often when I discover combinations that I normally wouldn't dream of putting on the same plate. When cilantro pesto and grilled-pineapple salsa fell together one afternoon when the staff was eating, I realized we were on to something. They have been happily married ever since.

1 ripe pineapple, peeled (see below)

2 tsp. sesame oil

1 tbsp. olive oil

1 small red bell pepper, diced

¼ cup cilantro, coarsely chopped

1 tbsp. chopped ginger

6 mahi-mahi fillets, 6-8 oz. each

Kosher salt

Olive oil

1 recipe Cilantro Pesto (see index)

To peel a pineapple, it is best to use a very sharp chef's knife or a serrated bread knife. Cut the bottom off of the pineapple to make a flat base so that it can stand on its own. Cut the green top off. Stand the pineapple upright (put your cutting board inside of a cookie sheet with sides so that you can catch all of the juices that run off). Beginning at the top of the pineapple, carefully slice the skin off from top to bottom, following the curve of the fruit as best you can. Be sure to remove all of the eyes.

Next, slice the pineapple into big slabs, about ¾ inch thick. Discard the core of the pineapple. Put the slices in a stainless-steel bowl and drizzle them with the oils. Add the reserved juices from the cutting board. Toss the pineapple slices around so that they are well coated with oil.

Place the pineapple slices on a preheated grill (reserve the juices in the bowl) and let them sit long enough to pick up some good grill marks. This can be done before, during, or after grilling something else. If you don't plan on grilling or if you don't want to fire up the grill just for this recipe, you can toss the pineapple on a hot griddle or even into a hot pan. While grilling is the best option (that's why it is called "grilled" pineapple salsa), the important thing is to caramelize the sugars. Remove the pineapple slices to the bowl and allow to cool. As the pineapple cools it will release some juices and you don't want to lose those.

Once the pineapple slices have cooled enough to handle, dice them into small chunks and toss them back into the bowl with the reserved juices. Add the pepper, cilantro, and ginger and mix well. The salsa can be made a day in advance, so if you happen to be grilling one night, throw on some pineapple for salsa the *next* night.

Dab the mahi-mahi fillets dry with a paper towel and season them on one side with a little kosher salt. Preheat a thick-bottomed sauté pan on the stovetop, add a drizzle of olive oil, and gently place the mahi, salted side down, into the pan. Cook over medium-high heat for about 5 minutes per side or until the fish is easily pierced with a metal skewer. To serve, drizzle each plate with a generous helping of the pesto, place the mahi-mahi on top, then plop a nice, big spoonful of the salsa on top of the fish. **Serves 6.**

Roasted Salmon with Miso Vinaigrette

Here is another good example of a vinaigrette being used on an entree instead of a salad. The savory sweet flavor of the miso works well with the richness of the salmon. Watercress adds a crispy bite to the dish.

3 tbsp. white miso paste

4 tbsp. rice vinegar

4 tbsp. mushroom-flavored soy sauce

1 tbsp. sesame oil

1 tbsp. sugar

2 cloves garlic, minced

1 tbsp. chopped ginger

1 cup olive oil

6 fillets salmon, 6-7 oz. each

Kosher salt

3 bunches fresh watercress

½ cup ginger-soy vinaigrette (see Spinach Salad recipe)

Place the miso paste, vinegar, soy sauce, and sesame oil in a stainless-steel bowl and whisk until smooth. Add the sugar, garlic, and ginger. Slowly whisk in the olive oil.

Place the salmon fillets onto a lightly oiled roasting pan and season them with a sprinkle of kosher salt. Put them on the middle rack of a 400-degree oven. Cook the fish for 10-12 minutes or until cooked to a medium doneness.

Toss the watercress with the ginger-soy vinaigrette in a stainless-steel bowl. Place a small mound of the watercress on the center of each plate. Top the watercress salad with a piece of fish and ladle the miso vinaigrette around the salad on the plate. **Serves 6.**

Gorgonzola and Walnut Crusted Salmon with Tomato-Herb Vinaigrette

Pairing cheese with fish is usually a culinary no-no, but there are exceptions to every rule. Salmon, especially a wild salmon like king or coho, has a rich enough flavor to stand up to a strong cheese like Gorgonzola. Walnuts are a great match for both the cheese and the salmon.

4 oz. Gorgonzola cheese

2 oz. unsalted butter, room temperature

½ cup toasted walnuts, chopped

6 fillets salmon, 6-7 oz. each

Kosher salt

Oil

In an electric mixer with the paddle attachment, cream together the cheese and butter until smooth. Fold in the walnuts with a rubber spatula until well incorporated.

Season the salmon fillets on one side with kosher salt, then place them, salted side down, in a preheated sauté pan that has been lightly oiled with olive oil. Cook the salmon until it begins to brown on one side, and then turn over. Remove the fish to a baking pan. Top each portion of salmon with about 2 tbsp. Gorgonzola and walnut topping and spread it evenly. Place in a preheated 400-degree oven for about 8 minutes or until the crust begins to brown.

Tomato-Herb Vinaigrette

2 vine-ripened tomatoes

½ cup fresh basil leaves, chopped

1 shallot, minced

Juice of 1 lemon

¼ cup rice vinegar

½ cup olive oil

Salt and pepper to taste

Core the tomatoes and cut an X in the bottom end of each, just deep enough to pierce the skin. Plunge the tomatoes in boiling water for 10 seconds to loosen the skin, then "shock" them in ice water until cool enough to handle. Starting at the X, peel the skin off using a paring knife. Cut the tomatoes in half through the equator and gently squeeze the seeds out. Coarsely chop the tomatoes and put them into a blender along with the basil, shallot, lemon juice, and vinegar. Puree until smooth and remove to a stainless-steel bowl. Whisk in the olive oil by hand. (If you puree the olive oil with the other ingredients, the vinaigrette will incorporate too much air and the color will turn lighter.) Season with salt and pepper.

Line each of 6 plates with the room-temperature vinaigrette. Top with the 6 fillets of salmon, garnish with a basil leaf if you like, and serve immediately. **Serves 6.**

Sautéed Salmon with Asian Vegetable and Wasabi-Pea Salad

When I am at work I seldom sit down to eat. One day I was so busy that I didn't have time to cook anything for myself, so I grabbed a handful of raw vegetables from the line, dressed them with a splash of ginger-soy vinaigrette, and walked out to the bar to check the reservation book. I sort of absentmindedly reached for a bowl of wasabi peas (which we serve as a bar snack) and dumped them in my raw-vegetable salad. This dish went onto the specials menu that very night.

I always feel healthier after eating this. The vegetables make for a colorful plate. The wasabi peas (to which I am hopelessly addicted) provide a fabulous crunch, and the vinaigrette perks up the whole dish. Since the vegetables in this recipe are presented raw, it is best to serve this in the summer when the squash and zucchini are at the peak of freshness. If the vegetables come from your own garden, so much the better.

2 medium zucchini

2 medium yellow squash

1 carrot, peeled

1 red bell pepper, seeded

6 fillets wild salmon, 6-7 oz. each

Kosher salt

2 tbsp. olive oil

1 cup wasabi peas

¾ cup ginger-soy vinaigrette (see Spinach Salad recipe)

Using the fine julienne blade on a mandoline, shred the zucchini, squash, and carrot into long strips. Julienne the pepper by hand. Toss the vegetables together.

Season the salmon fillets on one side with kosher salt. Preheat a heavy skillet over medium-high heat. Add the oil and gently place the salmon in, salted side down. Cook until golden brown on one side, then gently turn over and continue cooking. Cook to desired doneness. (If you do not have a skillet large enough to fit all the salmon at one time, you can partially cook the fillets in batches on one side, then place them on a baking pan and finish cooking them in the oven.)

Just before serving, place the vegetables and peas in a large bowl, add the vinaigrette, and toss until well coated. Place a pile of the vegetables in the center of each of 6 plates. Prop a fillet of salmon on top of the vegetable salad and serve immediately. **Serves 6.**

Wasabi Peas

This popular Asian bar snack is made from dried green peas that have been coated with a wasabi paste. They are crunchy, slightly spicy, and highly addictive. I like to add them to salads for extra crunch and flavor, but they are best eaten out of hand with a cold beer. Wasabi peas are available in Asian markets and some whole-foods stores.

Tortilla-Crusted Salmon with Roasted-Jalapeño Cream

I like fish with a crust or some kind of topping. The tortillas add a great crunch to this dish. The black beans and jalapeño cream work well with the tortilla crunch. This is a great dish with a cold Mexican beer.

8 corn tortillas

Oil for frying

1 tsp. chili powder, preferably ancho chile

½ tsp. salt

4 jalapeño peppers

1 tsp. minced garlic

½ cup sour cream

2 tbsp. half-and-half or milk

Salt to taste

6 fillets salmon, 6-7 oz. each

Kosher salt

2 tbsp. olive oil

Black beans and rice

Fry the tortillas in hot oil until crispy. Drain on absorbent paper and cool to room temperature. Crush the tortillas and place them in a food processor along with the chili powder and salt. Pulse the machine until the tortillas are pulverized.

Place the jalapeños in a dry pan over medium heat and roast them until the skins are charred and blistered on all sides. Remove from the heat and cool to room temperature. When cool, remove the stems, skins, and seeds and place the flesh in a blender along with the garlic, sour cream, and half-and-half. Puree until smooth, scraping the sides with a rubber spatula when necessary. Season to taste with salt and funnel the sauce into a squeeze bottle.

Season the salmon fillets with a sprinkle of kosher salt, and then dredge them in the ground tortillas until well coated. Place the salmon fillets into a hot skillet along with the olive oil. Cook on one side until the tortilla crust is nice and crispy. Turn the fillets over, reduce the heat to medium, and continue cooking until the fish is done to your liking. Plate the salmon and drizzle with a generous amount of the roasted-jalapeño cream. Serve with black beans and rice. **Serves 6.**

This is always a popular dish at Tsunami. The buttery, roasted macadamia nuts are a good balance for the unmistakable, earthy flavor of the shiitake mushrooms.

½ cup macadamia nuts

½ cup flour

1 lb. fresh shiitake mushrooms

Olive oil

4 tbsp. soy sauce

2 tsp. sugar

Juice of 1 lime

1 tbsp. chopped ginger

1 clove garlic, chopped

2 tsp. sesame oil

4 tbsp. rice vinegar

½ cup peanut oil

6 fillets mahi-mahi, 6-8 oz. each

Kosher salt

Cooked basmati or black Thai rice

Grind the macadamia nuts in a food processor along with the flour and set aside. Remove the stems from the shiitake mushrooms and slice the mushrooms thinly. Sauté the mushrooms in a little olive oil in a hot pan, just until soft. Set aside to cool.

To make the vinaigrette, place the soy sauce, sugar, and lime juice in a stainless-steel bowl and mix until the sugar dissolves. Add the ginger, garlic, sesame oil, and vinegar and mix well. Slowly drizzle in the peanut oil while whisking.

Season the mahi fillets on one side with kosher salt. Preheat a sauté pan, add 1 tbsp. olive oil, and place the fish in the pan, salted side down. Cook for 3-4 minutes and turn the fillets over.

Top each fillet with a coating of the macadamia nut flour, patting it down evenly. Place fish in a preheated 400-degree oven. Cook fillets until crust is a light golden brown.

Spread the sautéed shiitake mushrooms evenly over 6 plates. Top with a portion of fish, and then ladle 2 oz. vinaigrette around the fish. Serve immediately with a scoop of basmati or black Thai rice. **Serves 6.**

Cilantro-Crusted Mahi-Mahi

A lighter crust atop the mahi-mahi makes this recipe a great dish for a poolside lunch. It would be good with a citrus-based vinaigrette—perhaps even a Lobster Vinaigrette with Ginger and Scallions, if you're feeling a little decadent (see index).

2 cups *panko* (Japanese breadcrumbs)

1 packed cup cilantro, coarsely chopped

2 tbsp. soy sauce

5 tbsp. olive oil

6 fillets mahi-mahi, 6-7 oz. each

Kosher salt

Place the *panko* and cilantro into a large bowl and mix well with your hands. Add the soy sauce and 3 tbsp. oil. Rub the mixture together with your fingers until it holds together when squeezed.

Add the remaining oil to a hot sauté pan. Season the mahi-mahi fillets on one side with a little kosher salt and place them, salted side down, in the sauté pan. Cook for 3 minutes, then turn over. Top each fillet with about 2½ tbsp. cilantro mixture. Remove the mahi fillets to a baking sheet and place them in a 400-degree oven for 8-10 minutes or until the crust is slightly browned. **Serves 6.**

Roasted Grouper on Lentil Puree with Curry Oil

1 cup yellow lentils

4 cups water

1 clove garlic, minced

Salt and fresh-ground black pepper to taste

6 fillets grouper, 7-8 oz. each

Kosher salt

2 tbsp. olive oil

Curry Oil (see index)

Cilantro Rice (see index)

Place the lentils, water, and garlic into a medium saucepan over high heat. Bring to a boil, stirring frequently to keep the lentils from clumping together. Reduce to a low simmer, cover with a lid, and cook for 20-25 minutes or until tender. Season with salt and pepper and puree in blender. Keep warm until ready to serve.

Dab the grouper fillets dry with a paper towel, and then sprinkle on one side with kosher salt. Preheat a large sauté pan and the olive oil. Place the grouper in the pan, salted side down, and cook until golden brown on one side, then turn over and continue cooking until done when tested with a metal skewer.

Ladle the lentil puree on each of 6 warm plates. Top with the grouper, then drizzle the plate with the Curry Oil. Serve with Cilantro Rice. **Serves 6.**

Grouper Roasted in Rice Paper with Ginger and Cilantro

This dish is a little involved prepwise, but the results are impressive. Best of all, you can wrap the fish ahead of time and throw them in the oven just before you are ready to eat.

6 fillets grouper, about 6 oz. each

Salt and pepper

4 tbsp. olive oil

6 sheets rice paper

Warm water

6 sprigs fresh cilantro

3 or 4 oz. fresh ginger, peeled and finely julienned

Dab the grouper fillets dry with a paper towel and season on one side with salt and pepper. Preheat a large skillet, add 2 tbsp. oil, and place the fish in, salted side down. Cook until golden brown on one side. Remove from the pan and cool to room temperature.

Soak 1 sheet rice paper in a bowl of warm water until pliable. Remove from the water to a clean, dry work surface. Place 1 sprig cilantro, top side down, on the center of the paper. Top the cilantro with about 1 tbsp. ginger. Place 1 fillet, browned side down, on top of the ginger and cilantro in the center of the paper. Fold the bottom half of the rice paper up over the fish. Fold in the sides of the paper, and then fold over the top half of the rice paper to completely seal the fish. Repeat with the remaining fillets. At this point, the fish can be placed on a cookie sheet, covered with a barely damp towel, and kept in the refrigerator until you are ready to cook them.

To cook, preheat a skillet to medium hot, add the remaining oil, and then place the wrapped fish, cilantro side down, into the pan. Cook until the rice paper begins to brown slightly. Remove the wrapped fish from the skillet and place them, cilantro side up, onto a cookie sheet. Finish the fish in a preheated 400-degree oven until cooked through. (Use a metal skewer inserted into the fish to test for doneness.) **Serves 6.**

This hearty dish is a favorite of my wait staff, who claim that they need to taste it every time I offer it as a special. I must admit I am a bit partial to this dish as well. But I like practically anything with bacon on it. Sage, also, is one of the most underrated herbs, and I enjoy working with it.

6 fillets halibut, 6-7 oz. each

6 raw strips hickory-smoked or apple-wood-smoked bacon

1 clove garlic, minced

2 tbsp. olive oil

¼ cup small-diced carrot

¼ small-diced celery

½ cup small-diced onion

2 cups cooked white beans

½ cup chicken stock

2 bunches fresh watercress, rinsed

Salt and pepper to taste

1 recipe Sage Pesto (see index)

Pat the halibut fillets dry with a paper towel. Wrap each piece of fish with 1 strip bacon so that the loose ends wind up underneath the fish. Place a heavy roasting pan in a preheated 400-degree oven for 15 minutes. Remove the pan from the oven and place the fillets in the pan with the loose ends of the bacon facing up. Return the pan to the oven and cook until bacon is crisp on the bottom side. Turn the fish fillets over and continue cooking until fish is cooked through.

In a medium saucepan, cook the garlic in oil for 10 seconds. Add the carrot, celery, and onion and continue cooking for another 30 seconds, stirring. Add the white beans and stock, and stir until beans are warm. Add the watercress, cover the pan, remove from heat, and let stand for 1 minute. Season with salt and pepper.

Place a generous spoonful of the warm white bean salad on each of 6 plates. Remove the fish from the roasting pan using a slotted spatula and place a fillet on top of each portion of white beans. Top with a generous dollop of Sage Pesto and serve immediately. **Serves 6.**

Spicy Seafood Tostada with Smoked Chile Cream

We go through a lot of fish at Tsunami. Some days I filet and portion over one hundred pounds of fish. That makes for lots of leftover, odd-shaped pieces of fish that are just too small to do much of anything with. I started running the seafood tostada as a special once in a while to use up all the little bits of seafood. Before too long, people started asking about the tostada when they didn't see it on the menu. Now it has a permanent spot there.

I know that the average home cook doesn't have four or five different types of fish hanging around just waiting to be cooked. But the good thing about this dish is that you only have to have a couple of ounces of fish per portion. It is worth it just to buy a couple of different fish fillets to make this dish at home.

2 lb. assorted fish, cut into bite-sized pieces

1 tbsp. chili powder

½ tsp. cayenne

2 tbsp. peanut oil

3 tbsp. chipotles in adobo

4 oz. sour cream

Juice of 1 lime

4 tbsp. milk or half-and-half

1 cup chopped tomatoes

1 clove garlic, minced

4 tbsp. chopped cilantro

1 jalapeño pepper, seeded and minced

Salt and fresh-ground black pepper to taste

2 cups shredded lettuce

6 crisp tostada shells

1½ cups cooked black beans

Choose an assortment of fish with contrasting colors and textures. A few shrimp or bay scallops would be a nice addition as well. Toss all the fish bits in a bowl. Sprinkle with the chili powder and cayenne. Mix the fish bits until well coated with the seasonings.

Preheat a large skillet or sauté pan and add oil. Put the fish bits in the hot pan and let them cook without stirring for several minutes. Make sure that the pan is large enough to hold all of the fish without overcrowding.

Put the chipotles, sour cream, lime juice, and milk in a blender and puree until smooth. Funnel into a squeeze bottle and set aside. In a stainless-steel bowl, mix together the tomatoes, garlic, cilantro, and jalapeño. Season with salt and pepper and mix well.

Once the fish is cooked through, season with salt. Line each of 6 plates with lettuce. Put a tostada shell on top of the lettuce and a big spoonful of black beans on top of that. Evenly portion the cooked fish bits on top of the beans, top with a scoop of the tomato mixture, and then drizzle each plate with a generous amount of the chipotle cream. **Serves 6.**

Curry-Rubbed Salmon with Cucumber Raita

This East Indian-influenced dish has a good balance of hot and cold on the same plate. It goes against the principles drilled into me in culinary school, which dictate that everything on the same plate should be either all hot or all cold. Here's an example of why breaking the rules is sometimes a good thing.

½ cup peanut oil

3 tbsp. Madras curry powder

2 tsp. kosher salt

6 fillets salmon, 6-7 oz. each

2 cucumbers

1 small, ripe tomato, diced

½ jalapeño pepper, chopped

1 cup plain, whole-milk yogurt

¼ tsp. cumin seeds

4 or 5 sprigs cilantro, stems and leaves, chopped

Juice of 1 lemon

Salt to taste

Cooked basmati rice

Pour the oil into a wide, shallow baking dish. Sprinkle in the curry powder and kosher salt and add the salmon fillets. Roll the fish around in the oil until well coated, then allow to marinate for 30-40 minutes.

To make the raita, peel and seed the cucumbers and then either grate or dice them small depending on your preference. Place the cucumber in a stainless-steel bowl along with the tomato, jalapeño, and yogurt. Toast the cumin seeds by placing them in a heavy-duty skillet and heating them over medium heat until they begin to lightly smoke. It is best to toast a substantial amount of seeds at one time so that they are easier to grind. Once they are toasted and aromatic, grind the seeds to a fine powder using a mortar and pestle or an electric coffee grinder. Store any excess ground cumin in an airtight container and reserve it for another use. Add the cumin to the cucumber mixture. Add the cilantro and lemon juice and mix well. Season with salt.

Preheat a large sauté pan or skillet. Carefully place the salmon fillets in the hot pan. Since the fish is well coated with oil, it is not necessary to oil the pan. Cook the salmon until well browned, then turn over and continue cooking to medium doneness. Serve with a scoop of rice and a big dollop of the cucumber raita.
Serves 6.

Whole Fried Fish with Lemongrass and Garlic

Unless you have a commercial venta-hood in your kitchen at home, this is a dish you might want to consider cooking outdoors. While it is easy to prepare, it does create a lot of steam and a rather substantial aroma. But it also makes a striking centerpiece for a table full of people to share. Serve it with Chile-Soy Dipping Sauce and Green Papaya Salad or Asian Slaw.

1 whole fish (snapper, tilapia, or striped bass), about 2 lb.

1 tbsp. minced garlic

3 tbsp. chopped ginger

2 tbsp. chopped lemongrass

3 tbsp. soy sauce

2 tsp. crushed red pepper

1 tsp. sugar

1 tbsp. dry sherry

Peanut oil for frying

Flour for dredging

Cilantro sprigs

Jalapeño pepper slices

Cut green onions

If you plan on serving the fish head-on, have your fishmonger remove the gills. Otherwise, just cut the head off before cooking. Starting right behind the head, make 6 or 8 bone-deep, parallel cuts at an angle along the length of the fish. Make another series of cuts perpendicular to the first cuts. Do this on both sides of the fish.

Mix together the garlic, ginger, lemongrass, soy sauce, pepper, sugar, and sherry. Pulverize the mixture into a paste either in a blender or with a mortar and pestle. Pat the fish dry with paper towels, then rub all over with the paste, being sure to work it into the cavity and into all of the cuts. Allow the fish to marinate for at least 1 hour.

Preheat the oil to 350 degrees in an outdoor fish cooker or in a large pot on the stove. Wipe most of the marinade off the fish, dredge it in flour, and gently lower it into the hot oil. Cook for 12-15 minutes, turning once. Remove from the oil, being careful to keep it in one piece, and allow it to drain on absorbent paper. Serve on a large platter garnished with cilantro, jalapeño, and green onions.

shellfish

One of the good things about shellfish is that, with the exception of shrimp, you can purchase it live. Of course, as with any seafood, the less time between the ocean and the plate, the better. Shellfish offers almost as many options for cooking techniques as fin fish, but the simplest preparations are often the best.

Tsunami-Style Oysters Rockefeller

Scallop Carpaccio with Chile-Lime Vinaigrette

I think it's a shame to cook scallops. They have such a sweet, delicate flavor when they are raw that they don't need any embellishment. I also like citrus and chiles together, so this dish is a great combination for me. The key is to select the freshest scallops available.

1½ lb. very fresh sea scallops

Juice of 2 limes

Juice of 1 orange

2 Thai chiles, seeded and chopped

1 tsp. sugar

¼ cup champagne vinegar

Pinch salt

1 cup olive oil

1 tbsp. cilantro "chives" (chopped cilantro stems)

Cut the scallops into thin rounds about the thickness and diameter of a half-dollar. Lay the slices onto each of 6 chilled plates, making sure that the slices do not overlap. Keep plates in refrigerator until ready to serve.

Place the lime juice, orange juice, chiles, sugar, vinegar, and salt into a stainless-steel bowl and stir until the sugar dissolves. Slowly drizzle in the olive oil while whisking. Add the cilantro chives and whisk to incorporate. Just before serving, drizzle the scallops with the vinaigrette. Serve immediately. **Serves 6.**

Crab Cakes

1 lb. jumbo lump crabmeat

6 egg yolks

3 tbsp. mayonnaise

1 small red onion, diced small

2 cloves garlic, minced

4 tbsp. chopped cilantro

Juice and zest of 1 lemon

Breadcrumbs as needed

Peanut oil for frying

Pick through the crabmeat and discard any cartilage. Place the yolks, mayonnaise, onion, garlic, cilantro, and lemon juice and zest in a stainless-steel bowl and mix well. Add the crabmeat and very gently mix it in by hand, being careful not to break up the crabmeat. Add ½ cup breadcrumbs at a time and gently mix them in until the mixture holds together when you squeeze it. Form the mixture into individual balls and then mash them slightly to make cakes.

Preheat a large, thick-bottomed skillet and add enough oil to cover the bottom. Dredge the crab cakes in breadcrumbs, then place them in the hot oil. Cook until golden brown on both sides. Serve with Black Bean Remoulade or Wasabi Aioli (see index). **Serves 6.**

Crawfish Cakes with Black Bean Remoulade

Having grown up in the South, I find crawfish cakes every bit as logical as crab cakes. The best thing about this recipe is that you can leave the crawfish meat in big chunks and the cakes still hold together great without the addition of too much breadcrumb binder.

2 lb. cooked crawfish tail meat

2 tbsp. diced red bell peppers

2 tbsp. diced green bell peppers

3 tbsp. Dijon mustard

2 tbsp. horseradish

Juice of 1 lemon

1 egg

¼ cup heavy whipping cream

Panko (Japanese breadcrumbs) as needed

Salt and pepper to taste

Olive oil

Butter

Black Bean Remoulade

1 egg

2 egg yolks

2 tsp. dried or 1 tbsp. fresh tarragon

2 tsp. Dijon mustard

2 cloves garlic, minced

1 tbsp. chopped ginger

2 tsp. sambal

Juice of 1 lemon

¼ tsp. salt

1 cup olive oil

1 tbsp. Chinese black beans

2 tsp. capers, drained

Chop the crawfish meat coarsely and place in a stainless-steel bowl. Add the red bell pepper, green bell pepper, mustard, horseradish, lemon juice, egg, and cream. Mix together with hands until well incorporated. Add the *panko*, ½ cup at a time, until the mixture holds together when you squeeze it with your hands. Season with salt and pepper. Form the mixture into individual cakes, dredge in additional *panko*, and sauté in a mixture of oil and butter until golden brown on both sides.

Place the egg, yolks, tarragon, mustard, garlic, ginger, sambal, lemon juice, and salt in a food processor. Turn the machine on and run until the ingredients are well blended. With the machine running, slowly drizzle in the oil until it is all incorporated. Add the beans and capers and pulse the machine until they are mixed well into the sauce.

Serve the crawfish cakes with a dollop of remoulade. **Serves 6.**

Shrimp with Wasabi Cocktail Sauce

I know that shrimp cocktail is a bit dated. However, a friend of mine recently requested it at his wedding reception so I decided to give it a new twist. The addition of wasabi paste helps give the sauce a bit more of a nasal-clearing kick. It is definitely an improvement on an old standard.

1 gal. water

2 lemons, halved

2 tbsp. coriander seed

1 tbsp. crushed red pepper

2 lb. large shrimp, shell on

1 cup ketchup

Juice of 1 lemon

2 tbsp. horseradish

2 tbsp. wasabi powder, dissolved in 2 tbsp. water

1 tbsp. soy sauce

Bring water to boil in a large pot. Squeeze the halved lemons into the water and drop them in the pot along with the coriander and pepper. Return the water to a boil and add the shrimp. Cook until the shrimp are pink and firm. Drain and shock in ice water until completely cool.

Mix together the ketchup, lemon juice, horseradish, wasabi paste, and soy sauce and stir until well incorporated. Serve the shrimp on a chilled platter with the cocktail sauce in the middle. **Serves 6.**

Shrimp in Coconut Milk

2 tbsp. peanut oil

½ yellow onion, peeled and sliced thin

3 small cloves garlic, minced

2 tbsp. chopped ginger

2 lb. medium shrimp, peeled and deveined

1 cup coconut milk

2 tsp. sugar

1 tbsp. tamarind paste, dissolved in 2 tbsp. hot water

Cooked basmati rice

Preheat a large skillet and add oil. Add the onion slices, garlic, and ginger and sauté for about 30 seconds, stirring. Add the shrimp and cook until they begin to turn pink. Add the coconut milk, sugar, and tamarind liquid and allow the shrimp to simmer until cooked through. Serve immediately with a scoop of rice. Serves 6.

Hot and Pungent Shrimp

4 jalapeño peppers, seeded and coarsely chopped

¼ cup mushroom-flavored soy sauce

1 tbsp. chopped ginger

2 cloves garlic, minced

1 tbsp. olive oil

2½ lb. medium shrimp, peeled and deveined

2 cups coconut milk

3 green onions, sliced

Cooked basmati rice

Place the jalapeño peppers, soy sauce, ginger, and garlic in a blender and puree until smooth. Preheat a large skillet and add oil. Cook the shrimp until they begin to turn pink.

Add the coconut milk and bring to a boil. Add the chile puree, one spoonful at a time, until it reaches the desired heat level. (Since jalapeño peppers have such an unpredictable spice level, it's hard to know how much to add unless you taste occasionally.) Add green onions. Simmer the shrimp until they are cooked through. Serve immediately with a scoop of rice. **Serves 8.**

Grilled Shrimp with Lemongrass and Fish Sauce

4 tbsp. minced lemon-grass

1 tbsp. sugar

2 tbsp. soy sauce

1 tbsp. fish sauce

2 cloves garlic, minced

2 tbsp. olive oil

2 lb. large shrimp, head and shell on

Mix together the lemongrass, sugar, soy sauce, fish sauce, and garlic in a spice grinder or a mortar. Grind into a paste and add the olive oil. Toss the paste with the shrimp until well coated. Allow the shrimp to marinate for 2-3 hours.

Place the shrimp on a hot grill and cook on one side until they begin to turn pink. Turn over and continue cooking until done. Serve with a side of Green Papaya Salad (see index) and a cold beer. **Serves 6 as an appetizer.**

2 cups ice-cold water

1 egg yolk

1 cup cornstarch

1 cup all-purpose flour

Peanut oil for frying

1 lb. medium shrimp, peeled and deveined, tails attached

Additional all-purpose flour for dredging

With a pair of chopsticks, stir together the water and yolk in a medium stainless-steel bowl. Add the cornstarch and stir in with the chopsticks. Add the flour and stir with the chopsticks until just blended. The batter should be slightly lumpy and the consistency of a thin crepe batter. Keep the batter ice cold until ready to use.

Preheat an electric wok or fryer to 350 degrees. Make sure the oil is at least 3 inches deep. Butterfly the shrimp, and then dredge them in the flour. Shake off the excess flour and dip the shrimp in the tempura batter, holding them by the tail. Still holding the shrimp by the tail, lower them slowly into the hot oil. Gently swirl each shrimp around in the oil until it begins to float, before letting go of the tail. Tempura is a light batter, so you cannot judge doneness by the color. Let the shrimp cook until the batter looks good and crisp on the outside, then remove one from the oil to test for doneness. Drain the shrimp on absorbent paper and keep the cooked ones in a warm oven until they are all cooked. **Makes 20 to 25 pieces.**

Shrimp Tempura

This recipe is a bit more involved than the previous one, but it makes a beautiful, lacy finished product.

1 cup water

¼ cup cornstarch

2 cups crushed ice

½ cup additional corn-starch

2 tbsp. baking powder

1 tsp. salt

¼ tsp. ground white pepper

1 tbsp. sugar

Peanut oil for frying

1 lb. medium shrimp, peeled and deveined

All-purpose flour for dredging

Mix together the water and ¼ cup cornstarch. Bring to boil in a medium saucepan, stirring constantly to keep smooth. The mixture will turn into a thick paste.

Remove the pan from the heat and add the crushed ice. (You can make crushed ice by placing ice cubes in a chilled food processor and pulsing it. Or wrap ice cubes in dishcloth and crush it with a meat mallet or a hammer.) Stir until the ice melts.

Mix together the ½ cup corn starch, baking powder, salt, white pepper, and sugar. Add the dry ingredients to the liquid ingredients and stir with a pair of chopsticks. Keep batter ice cold until ready to use. Follow the method for cooking the shrimp in the previous recipe. **Makes 20 to 25 pieces.**

Pan-Roasted Sea Scallops with Sweet-Corn Puree and Cilantro Pesto

2 cups vegetable or chicken stock

1 cup half-and-half

2 cups fresh corn kernels

1 tbsp. sugar

Salt and fresh-ground black pepper to taste

24 sea scallops, about 2½ lb.

2 tbsp. olive oil

1 recipe Cilantro Pesto (see index)

Cooked rice

Being the stock and half-and-half to a boil in a medium saucepan. Add the corn and sugar and cook 6-8 inutes or until corn is tender. Remove from heat and puree the liquid and corn all together in the blender. Season with salt and pepper and keep the puree warm until ready to use.

Pat scallops dry with a paper towel and season on one side with salt and pepper. Preheat a heavy skillet on the stove, add oil, and gently place the scallops in the pan, salted side down. Cook scallops until golden brown on side, then place the pan in a preheated 400-degree oven for 8-10 minutes. (If you don't have a pan large enough to hold all of the scallops at one time, use 2 pans or cook the scallops in batches and keep warm in the oven on a baking sheet.)

To serve, ladle a generous amount of the corn puree onto each of 6 warm plates. Place 4 large dollops Cilantro Pesto around each plate. Place 1 scallop on top of each dollop of pesto, slightly offset. Serve a scoop of rice right in the middle. **Serves 6.**

Oysters on the Half-Shell with Ginger Mignonette Sauce

I love raw oysters, but I think it is an abomination to slather them with cocktail sauce. I much prefer this simple concoction. It is much more respectful of the delicate flavor of the oyster. "Mignonette" is a French term for coarsely ground pepper.

½ cup sake

½ cup rice vinegar

1 large shallot, minced

1 tbsp. chopped ginger

Fresh-cracked black pepper to taste

3 doz. unshucked oysters, scrubbed

Heat the sake in a small saucepan to burn off the alcohol. Allow sake to cool, then add the rice vinegar, shallot, and ginger. Add black pepper to taste. Turn the oysters so that the curved side is down in order to reserve the juices, and then shuck them. Serve them on a platter of crushed ice. Serve the sauce in individual bowls for each person. **Serves 6.**

Tsunami-Style Oysters Rockefeller

This variation on a classic American dish gets a nice kick from sambal and enough lemongrass infusion to distinguish this Rockefeller from the original.

6 oz. unsalted butter

½ yellow onion, diced small

¼ cup chopped lemongrass

2 tbsp. chopped ginger

½ cup sake

2 tbsp. sambal

1 lb. fresh spinach leaves, chopped

¼ tsp. ground aniseed

1 cup *panko* bread-crumbs

½ cup grated Parmesan cheese

2 doz. unshucked oysters

Rock salt

Melt butter in a medium saucepan. Add the onion and cook until soft. Add the lemongrass and ginger and stir for 10 seconds. Add the sake, sambal, and spinach. Stir until the spinach has wilted down. Add aniseed, *panko*, and cheese. Stir until the cheese has melted, then remove from heat. Spread the mixture out on a baking pan and put in the refrigerator until cool.

Shuck the oysters, retaining as much of their natural juices as possible. Top each oyster with enough of the Rockefeller filling to completely cover the oyster. Spread a thick layer of rock salt onto a baking pan large enough to hold all of the oysters. Place the oysters on top of the rock salt, nestling the oyster shells into the salt to keep them steady. Place the oysters into a preheated 400-degree oven for about 15 minutes or until the oysters are bubbling around the edges. Serve on plates lined with rock salt. **Serves 4 to 6.**

Panko-Breaded Oysters with Curry Beurre Blanc

2 doz. large shucked oysters

1 cup all-purpose flour

3 cups *panko* (Japanese breadcrumbs)

3 eggs beaten with 2 tbsp. water

Peanut oil for frying

Curry Beurre Blanc

1 tbsp. minced shallot

3 sticks unsalted butter, cut into cubes

½ tsp. Madras curry powder

½ cup white wine

⅓ cup heavy whipping cream

Set up a breading station for the oysters. Place the flour and *panko* in separate, wide, shallow containers. Put the eggs in a medium stainless-steel bowl. Line up all of your ingredients as follows: container of oysters on the far left, the flour container just to the right of the oysters, the beaten eggs to the right of the flour, the *panko* to the right of the eggs, then a baking pan lined with wax paper on the far right. This is the proper breading technique no matter what you are coating with crumbs. With your left hand, drop 5 or 6 oysters into the flour at a time. Shake the pan until the oysters are well dusted with the flour. With your *right* hand transfer the oysters from the flour to the eggs, shaking off the excess flour. Swirl the oysters around in the eggs. With your *left* hand, remove the oysters from the eggs and drop them into the *panko* so that the oysters are not touching one another. Shake the pan until the oysters are well coated with the *panko*. With your *right* hand, remove the oysters to the pan lined with wax paper. The idea here is that you keep one hand dry and one hand wet. Otherwise you end up with your fingers breaded as well.

In a medium saucepan, cook the shallots in 1 tbsp. butter until soft. Add the curry powder and stir for 10 seconds. Add the wine and cook until the wine has reduced by half of its volume. Add the cream and cook until the liquid has reduced by half. Whisk in the remaining butter, one piece at a time, until it is all incorporated. Keep warm until ready to use.

Preheat a wok with 4 inches peanut oil to about 350 degrees or until a bamboo chopstick sizzles when dipped in the oil. Fry the oysters 6 at a time until golden brown. Drain on absorbent paper and keep the cooked oysters warm in a 200-degree oven until they are all cooked. Serve with the Curry Beurre Blanc. **Serves 6.**

Sake-Steamed Mussels in Thai Red-Curry Sauce

I have been serving this dish as an appetizer at Tsunami since the day we opened. Nearly everyone who orders the mussels asks for extra bread to sop up the sauce in the bottom of the bowl. While the sauce goes well with other seafood, I like the balance of the sake-scented shellfish with the spicy-sweet curry sauce. This is great with a glass of Riesling.

1 can unsweetened coconut milk

2 stalks fresh lemon-grass, white part only, minced

½ cup fresh basil leaves, lightly packed

½ cup light brown sugar

1 tbsp. Thai fish sauce

2 tbsp. chopped ginger

2½ tbsp. Thai red curry paste

2 lb. fresh black mussels in shells

¼ cup sake

Place the coconut milk, lemongrass, basil, brown sugar, fish sauce, and ginger in a heavy saucepan. Bring to a boil, reduce to a simmer, and cook for 10-15 minutes, stirring occasionally. Place the curry paste in a stainless-steel bowl. Ladle 1 cup hot liquid in the bowl and stir until the curry paste is smooth. Using a rubber spatula, scrape the curry paste back into the saucepan with the coconut milk. Continue cooking at a low simmer for another 15 minutes. Strain through a fine sieve and keep warm while you steam the mussels.

Scrub and debeard mussels and place in a wide-mouthed pot with a tight-fitting lid. Add the sake, bring to a boil, and then cover the pan. Steam the mussels for about 5 minutes or until they are open. Discard any unopened mussels. Drain off the excess liquid, or remove the mussels using a wire-meshed scoop. Divide the mussels equally among 4 bowls, top with a generous ladle of the curry sauces and serve immediately with lots of bread for sopping. **Serves 4.**

Pan-Seared Sea Scallops with Smoked-Tomato Beurre Blanc and Basil Oil

I put this dish on the menu one summer when I had a surplus of Ripley tomatoes. I was running out of things to do with tomatoes, so I decided to smoke a bunch of them and freeze the puree for the winter months. Well, this dish was so popular that I used up all the puree in the freezer and had to get more tomatoes. Now I make sure that I stock up on tomatoes so we have plenty of smoked-tomato puree for the winter.

When choosing scallops, make sure you buy "dry" scallops (scallops that have not been infused with a brine solution). Only "dry" scallops will give you the wonderful crust when seared in a hot pan.

2 large, vine-ripened tomatoes, halved and seeded

¼ cup dry white wine

1 large shallot, minced

¼ cup heavy whipping cream

½ lb. chilled, unsalted butter, cut into tbsp.-sized cubes

Salt and pepper to taste

½ cup fresh basil leaves

Boiling salted water

¼ cup olive oil

24 large sea scallops, about 2½ lb.

2 tbsp. olive oil

Cooked basmati rice

Place the tomatoes, cut side up, in a shallow roasting pan or a pie tin to catch all the juices. Using the wood chips of your choice, start a medium-hot grill. When it is ready, bank the coals and set the tomato pan on the cool side of the grill. Smoke until the tomatoes begin to soften and the skin peels off easily. Remove from the grill and pull the skins off. Puree the tomatoes in a blender and set aside. (The puree freezes beautifully, so make a huge batch and keep some for the future.)

Place the white wine and shallots in a thick-bottomed saucepan and bring to a boil. Cook until the wine has nearly evaporated. Add the smoked-tomato puree and the cream and cook until the liquid has reduced to about a third of its volume. Whisk the chilled cubes of butter into the sauce one at a time. Continue whisking until all the butter is incorporated. Salt to taste. Set the sauce aside on a warm, not hot, place on the stove.

Blanch the basil in the water for 10 seconds. Strain and rinse the basil in cold water. Squeeze out the excess water and chop. Place the basil with the ¼ cup oil in a blender and puree. Strain through a fine sieve and put the oil into a squeeze bottle.

Dab the scallops dry with a paper towel and season them liberally on one side with salt and pepper. (If the scallops have any excess moisture on top, they will steam in the pan and will not develop a good crust.) Preheat a large cast-iron skillet (or other thick-bottomed pan) until smoking hot. Add the 2 tbsp. olive oil, then gently place the scallops in the pan, salted side down. Cook the scallops until golden brown on the bottom, then turn them over with a pair of tongs and continue cooking to the desired doneness (medium-rare to medium is best). (If you don't have a pan large enough to fit all of the scallops at one time, use 2 pans or cook the scallops in batches and keep them on a baking sheet in a warm oven.)

To serve, ladle enough sauce on each of 6 plates to cover the surface. Place 4 scallops around the edge of each plate and drizzle with the Basil Oil. Serve with a scoop of rice in the middle. **Serves 6.**

meats

Fran Lebowitz said, "My favorite animal is steak." Man cannot live on fish alone. Well, he could, but it's nice to have a little variety. The recipes in this chapter are a departure from the average meat and potatoes.

Szechwan Lamb Chops with Sweet-Potato Risotto

Szechwan Lamb Chops with Sweet-Potato Risotto

The hint of sweetness that the hoisin sauce provides is a great match with the sweet gaminess of the lamb, especially New Zealand lamb, which tends to be milder than its American or Australian counterparts. This is not a risotto in the true sense of the word. However, the cooking method and the result are reminiscent of risotto. Unless your knife skills are good, a mandoline is indispensable for this recipe. It is important that the sweet potatoes are diced into a small, consistent size so that they cook uniformly.

2 racks of lamb, 8 bones each

¼ cup white miso paste

⅔ cup hoisin sauce

1½ tbsp. chopped ginger

2 cloves garlic, minced

2 tbsp. sake

2 tbsp. soy sauce

2 tsp. sugar

1 tbsp. sambal

Sweet-Potato Risotto

2 sweet potatoes, peeled

2 cups heavy whipping cream

1 pod star anise

Salt to taste

Have your butcher french the lamb racks for you. Trust me, you don't want to do this yourself. Mix together the miso paste, hoisin sauce, ginger, garlic, sake, soy sauce, sugar, and sambal and whisk until smooth. Slather the lamb racks with the Szechwan marinade and allow to sit overnight.

Preheat the oven to 400 degrees. Place the lamb racks on a roasting pan with the bones interlaced and place on the middle rack of the oven. Roast for 20-25 minutes. Remove the lamb from the oven and allow the meat to "rest" for about 10 minutes before cutting into individual chops. Cooking time will vary depending on the type of lamb you use. American and Australian lamb chops tend to be larger than those from New Zealand.

To make the risotto, cut the potatoes into cubes no larger than your pinky nail. If using a mandoline, first cut the potatoes into *batonettes* (French-fry shapes), then line up the *batonettes* and cut into small cubes. Place the potatoes, cream, and star anise into a saucepan and bring to a boil. Reduce the heat to a simmer and cook, stirring constantly, until the potatoes are tender, about 10 minutes. Season with salt. Cover and keep warm until ready to plate. Remove the star anise before serving. Serve the risotto alongside the chops. **Serves 4.**

Miso-Marinated Pork Tenderloin

Marinating serves the combined purposes of flavoring, tenderizing, and preserving a cut of meat. In this recipe, the main goal is to add flavor, since this is already a tender cut. This marinade has good "stickability" properties so that when you cook the pork, the marinade chars on the outside. This is a good thing.

4 tbsp. white miso paste

2 tbsp. sugar

½ cup sake

2 tbsp. chopped ginger

3 cloves garlic, minced

2 tbsp. soy sauce

4 pork tenderloins

Stir-fried bok choy

Cooked basmati rice

Mix together the miso paste, sugar, sake, ginger, garlic, and soy sauce and stir until smooth. Place the pork tenderloins in a single layer in a glass dish. Pour the marinade over the tenderloins and roll them around until well coated. Cover with plastic wrap and place in the refrigerator overnight, turning the tenderloins every 8 hours.

Grill the tenderloins on a medium-hot grill until charred on all sides. Move the tenders to the "cool" side of the grill, cover the grill, and let them cook to medium doneness (or more, depending on your taste). Remove them from the grill and let rest for 5 minutes, then slice. Serve them with bok choy and a scoop of rice. **Serves 4.**

Szechwan Eggplant with Pork

2 tbsp. peanut oil

1 lb. ground pork

1 bunch green onions, sliced

5 cloves garlic, minced

1 tbsp. ginger

4 lb. eggplant, cut into french-fry shapes about the size of your index finger

½ cup rice vinegar

2 tbsp. sugar

2 tbsp. Dragon Juice (see index)

Salt and pepper to taste

Cooked rice

Heat a wok or large sauté pan. Add oil, then pork. Cook until brown, stirring constantly to break up the meat. Drain off the excess fat.

Add green onions, garlic, and ginger and stir-fry for 30 seconds. Add the eggplant, stir, and cover the pan. Cook until the eggplant is soft, then add the vinegar, sugar, and Dragon Juice. Season with salt and pepper. Serve with a scoop of rice. **Serves 8.**

Asian-Brined Pork Tenderloin

Brining is an ancient method of preserving foods. It also tenderizes and adds succulence, especially to leaner cuts of meat. Because of these benefits, the technique of brining survives today. It is a simple and effective way to vastly improve any cut of meat.

2 qt. water

½ lb. kosher salt

1 tbsp. sugar

3 star anise pods

1 tbsp. whole black peppercorns

1 bunch green onions

5 slices fresh ginger, smashed

2 pork tenderloins, 1 to 1½ lb. each

To make the brine, bring water, salt, sugar, star anise, and peppercorns to a boil. Stir until salt and sugar dissolve. Remove from heat, cool, and add green onions and ginger slices.

Place pork tenderloins in a clean, nonreactive container and pour the cooled brine on top. Weight the tenderloins down so they are completely submerged in the brine. Cover container with plastic wrap and place in refrigerator for 3 to 7 days.

When you are ready to cook them, remove the tenderloins, rinse in cold water, and discard the brine. Since no further seasoning is needed, simply cook the pork in whatever manner you desire. **Serves 6.**

Asian-Brined Double-Cut Pork Chops with Peach Chutney

6 thick pork chops, 2 bones each

1 small yellow onion, diced

2 tsp. olive oil

1 tbsp. chopped ginger

1 clove garlic, minced

1 jalapeño pepper, seeded and sliced thin

2½ lb. ripe peaches, pitted and sliced

½ cup champagne vinegar

½ cup light brown sugar

Follow the recipe for Asian brine in the previous recipe. Submerge pork chops in the brine. Place in refrigerator, covered, for 3 days.

To make the chutney, sauté the onions briefly in oil in a nonreactive saucepan. Add ginger, garlic, and jalapeño and cook, stirring, for 2 minutes. Add peaches and cook for 1 or 2 minutes, stirring. Add vinegar and sugar, bring to a boil, and reduce to a simmer. Cook until peaches are quite soft, stirring occasionally. Remove from heat and cool.

Remove pork chops from brine, rinse them in cold water, and discard the brine. Since no further seasoning is necessary, place the pork chops directly onto a medium-hot grill and cook to medium doneness. Serve with a generous helping of peach chutney. **Serves 6.**

Mixed Grill with Crawfish Hash

This hearty dish is a bit of a challenge for one person to pull off alone. It is best if you have one person on the grill and another person making the hash. That way you are not dividing yourself between two different cooking stations.

1 rack of lamb, frenched and cut into 8 chops

Olive oil

Kosher salt and fresh-ground black pepper to taste

16 large sea scallops, about 1½-2 lb.

1 lb. large shrimp, peeled and deveined

8 pieces good-quality sausage (andouille, bratwurst, kielbasa, Italian)

2 Idaho potatoes, peeled

1 yellow onion, diced small

2 ribs celery, diced small

2 carrots, peeled and diced small

2 cloves garlic, minced

1 lb. cooked crawfish tail meat

1 cup chicken stock

2 tbsp. chopped fresh thyme

Prepare a charcoal grill and bank the coals so that you have a hot side and a not-so-hot side. Lightly coat the lamb chops with olive oil and season them with salt and pepper. Lay the scallops out on a clean work surface in pairs. Skewer the scallops together in pairs to make 8 portions. Use 2 skewers through each pair of scallops, otherwise the scallops will spin on the skewer and you will have a hard time turning them on the grill. Skewer the shrimp, 2 to a skewer, lengthwise, making 8 portions. Season the shrimp and scallop skewers with salt and pepper.

Make sure the grill is nice and hot. Wipe the grids with a lightly oiled rag, then place the lamb chops onto the hot side of the grill. Next add the sausages, also on the hot side of the grill. Place the shrimp and scallop skewers onto the not-so-hot side of the grill.

Cook lamb chops to desired doneness, turning once. Cook sausages until thoroughly heated. Cook shrimp until pink. Cook scallops until they get good grill marks on both sides. The scallops are best when they are not cooked all the way through. Remove everything to a clean roasting pan and keep warm.

To make the crawfish hash, dice the potatoes into small, consistently sized cubes. (This is when a mandoline comes in handy. By slicing the potatoes into fries first, it is an easy task to then cut them into perfect cubes.) In a large, deep skillet, cook the potatoes in ½ inch hot olive oil until golden brown on all sides. Remove the potatoes and set aside. Drain off the excess oil, leaving about 2 tbsp. Add the onion, celery, and carrot and stir well. Add the garlic and cook, stirring, until the vegetables begin to soften slightly. Add the crawfish, stock, and thyme. Bring the stock to a boil. Add the potatoes and season with salt and pepper.

Portion the hash evenly among 8 plates. On each plate arrange 1 lamb chop, 1 sausage, 1 shrimp skewer, and 1 scallop skewer. Serve immediately. **Serves 8.**

Smoked Duck Breast with Roasted-Eggplant Relish

Oftentimes it is difficult to coordinate a grilled dinner and get everything to the table hot. That is why I enjoy this dish so much. It is better served at room temperature, and without the rush to serve everything hot, the timing becomes very simple. While the eggplant is roasting you can start up the grill. While the duck is smoking you can make the relish. And while your neighbors are running back and forth trying to coordinate the grilling of the steaks to the tossing of the salad, you can be pouring yourself a glass of pinot noir and sitting down to a simple summer dinner. A side of rice and a bowl of Green Papaya Salad (see index) would round out the meal nicely.

1 large eggplant
¼ cup cilantro, chopped
1 clove garlic, minced
1 tbsp. chopped ginger
2 tsp. Thai fish sauce
2 tbsp. soy sauce
3 green onions, sliced
3 tbsp. diced red bell pepper
Salt and fresh-ground black pepper to taste
6 boneless duck breasts, about 2½-3 lb.

Cut the eggplant in half lengthwise after first removing the stem end. Lay the eggplant halves, cut side down, on a lightly oiled roasting pan. Roast the eggplant in a preheated 350-degree oven for 20 minutes or until the eggplant is soft. Remove from the oven and allow to cool slightly. Using a large serving spoon, scrape the pulp out of the eggplant and discard the skin. Chop the eggplant coarsely and place in a stainless-steel bowl. Add the cilantro, garlic, ginger, fish sauce, soy sauce, green onions, and bell pepper and mix well. Season with salt and pepper.

Trim any excess fat off the duck breasts. Score the skin by making 5 or 6 cuts through the skin. Place the duck breasts, skin side down, on the "cool" side of a moderately hot grill with the coals banked. Add chips of your choice and allow the duck to smoke until cooked to medium doneness. Remove from grill to a cutting board. Slice each breast into 5 or 6 slices. Place a generous portion of eggplant on 6 plates. Arrange the duck slices around the eggplant and serve. **Serves 6.**

Roasted Duck Breast with Shiitake-Mushroom Risotto

1 lb. fresh shiitake mushrooms, with stems on

5 cups vegetable or chicken stock

2 tbsp. olive oil

2 cloves garlic, minced

½ cup small-diced yellow onion

1½ cups arborio rice

6 duck breasts

Salt and pepper to taste

2 tbsp. chopped chives

Remove the stems from the mushrooms. Add the stems to the stock and bring to a boil. Reduce the heat low enough to keep the stock hot but not simmering. Allow the stems to steep for 15 minutes, and then strain the stock. Keep warm.

Slice the shiitake mushrooms thinly. Place the oil, garlic, shiitake mushrooms, and onion in a heavy, thick-bottomed saucepan. Cook until the onion begins to soften, stirring occasionally. Add the rice and stir until well coated with oil. Stir 1 cup hot stock into the rice. Cook, stirring constantly, until all of the liquid has been absorbed by the rice. Continue this process until all the stock has been used. Keep the risotto warm while you cook the duck.

Slash the skin of the duck breasts 4 or 5 times all the way through to the flesh. This allows the fat to seep out of the skin so that it will crisp up when it cooks. Season the duck breasts with salt and pepper and place them skin side down in a hot, un-oiled sauté pan. Cook until the skin begins to brown, then place the pan in a preheated 400-degree oven and cook until the skin on the breasts is evenly browned. Turn the duck over and continue cooking until about medium rare.

Remove from the oven, pour a little bit of the pan drippings into the risotto, and allow the duck breasts to "rest" for 5 minutes. Add the chives to the risotto and stir well. Portion the risotto evenly onto 6 plates. Slice the duck breasts into thin slices and fan them around the risotto. **Serves 6.**

2 tsp. kosher salt

2 pods star anise, crushed

2 tsp. Chinese five-spice powder

1 green onion, sliced

2 tsp. chopped ginger

1 tbsp. sake

12 semiboneless quail

2 lb. red cabbage, sliced coleslaw style

½ lb. Chinese sausage, cooked and diced small (see sidebar)

1 tbsp. sesame oil

1 cup toasted walnuts

1 tsp. minced garlic

2 tbsp. soy sauce

¼ cup rice vinegar

½ cup chicken or vegetable stock

Salt to taste

Additional soy sauce for rubbing

Flour for dredging

Peanut oil for frying

Steaming Seasonings

Small handful star anise

½ bunch green onions

4-5 slices ginger, smashed

Mix together the salt, star anise, five-spice powder, green onion, ginger, and sake to make a marinade. Generously rub the quail with the marinade and allow to marinate for at least 2 hours. Set up a steamer using a large wok or a hotel pan steamer as described in the Ginger-Steamed Snapper recipe (see index). Place steaming seasonings into the water. Once the quail have marinated, bring the steamer to a boil, place the quail on a plate (if using a wok) or in a perforated pan (if using a hotel pan steamer), and cover with a lid. Steam the quail for 10 minutes, then remove from steamer and allow to cool to room temperature.

In a large stainless-steel bowl, toss together the cabbage, sausage, sesame oil, walnuts, garlic, soy sauce, and vinegar until the cabbage is well coated. Preheat a large skillet over high heat. Add the cabbage and cook, stirring frequently until the cabbage, begins to wilt. Add the stock, reduce the heat to low, and cover. Cook for an additional 5 minutes. Season to taste with salt.

Wipe excess marinade off of the quail, then rub them with a light coating of soy sauce. Dredge the quail in flour, shake off the excess flour, and fry them in peanut oil until the skin is crisp and golden brown. Serve 2 quail per person on a bed of the braised red cabbage. **Serves 6.**

Chinese Sausage

This thin, dense, fatty pork sausage has a rich, sweet flavor. It is a great addition to stir-fried dishes, soups, or even scrambled eggs (perhaps that's just me). At any rate, it is a unique and altogether delicious sausage. It can be found in Asian markets (naturally), where it is sometimes known as lop chong.

Chicken Katsu

This dish is a variation of *Tonkatsu,* a fried, breaded pork cutlet. *Katsu* is the Japanization of the word "cutlet."

Dipping Sauce

1 cup ketchup

2 tsp. dry mustard

1 tsp. sugar

1 tsp. hot sauce

1 tbsp. Worcestershire sauce

2 tbsp. chicken or vegetable stock

Chicken

6 boneless, skinless chicken breasts

Salt and fresh-ground black pepper to taste

All-purpose flour for dredging

2 eggs beaten with 2 tbsp. water

2 cups *panko* (Japanese breadcrumbs)

Peanut oil for frying

Mix all sauce ingredients together and set aside.

Trim the chicken breasts of any excess fat or cartilage. Place them between 2 sheets of plastic wrap and pound them to a ¼-inch thickness using a meat mallet or the flat side of a Chinese cleaver. Season the breasts with salt and pepper. Dredge in flour and dip into the egg wash, then into the *panko,* lightly packing on the crumbs with your hand.

Preheat a large, heavy skillet, add about 1 inch oil, and heat until a bamboo chopstick sizzles when you stick it in the oil. Gently place the breaded chicken breasts into the hot oil, being careful not to overcrowd the pan. (You may have to cook the chicken in batches, in which case you may keep the cooked portions in a warm oven until they are all done.) Fry until golden brown on one side, then turn over and continue cooking until golden brown all over. Serve immediately with individual bowls of the dipping sauce. **Serves 6.**

Grilled Filet of Beef with Smoked-Chile Butter

This has been a staple of the Tsunami menu since 1998. I have tried other cuts of beef and other preparations, but popular demand keeps insisting that I don't change this dish.

1 7-oz. can chipotles in adobo

Juice of 1 lime

1 lb. unsalted butter, room temperature

6 filets beef tenderloin, 8 oz. each

½ tsp. salt

Ice water

Place the chipotles and lime juice in blender and puree until smooth. Put the butter into the bowl of an electric mixer. With the paddle attachment, whip the butter until fluffy. Add the chipotle puree and continue whipping, on low speed, until the puree is incorporated thoroughly. Stop the machine occasionally to scrape the sides and bottom with a rubber spatula.

Lay out a 14-18-inch strip of wax paper horizontally on a work surface. Place the softened chipotle butter in an even mound across the length of the wax paper. Fold the top edge of the wax paper over the butter towards you. Holding the two edges of the wax paper in front of you, use a sturdy cookie sheet with a rolled edge to push up against the butter. This will form the butter into a perfect tube. Roll the butter up the rest of the way in the wax paper and store in the refrigerator until ready to use.

Season the beef filets on one side with salt and place on a moderately hot grill, salted side down. Cook to desired doneness, turning once. While the filets are grilling, take the tube of butter out of the refrigerator. It should be firm enough to slice. Cut 6 coin-shaped slices from the butter tube, cutting right through the wax paper. Peel the wax paper off the butter slices and place them in a small container of ice water. Wrap the surplus butter in aluminum foil, label with a permanent marker, and freeze for later use.

Once the filets are done, remove them from the grill and plate them. Just before serving, place 1 round chipotle butter on top of each hot filet. By the time the plates get to the table, the butter will have melted, leaving a wonderful smoky, spicy glaze on the filets. **Serves 6.**

Spice-Rubbed Grilled Flank Steak on Black Beans

6 tbsp. olive oil

Juice of 1 lime

1 tbsp. ground cumin

2 tbsp. chili powder, preferably ancho chile

2 tsp. ground allspice

2 tsp. fresh-ground black pepper

1 tsp. kosher salt

3 lb. flank steak

3 cups cooked black beans (see index)

Warm corn tortillas

In a stainless-steel bowl, mix together the oil, lime juice, cumin, chili powder, allspice, pepper, and salt to make a paste. Coat the steak well with the paste by rubbing it on with your hands. Allow the steak to sit for an hour or so while you prepare a hot grill.

Once the coals are ready, place the steak on the grill and cook 4 to 6 minutes on each side. Remove from the grill and allow the steak to "rest" for 6 to 8 minutes before slicing. With a long, sharp knife, cut the steak across the grain (the grain runs lengthwise on a flank steak) into slices about ¼ inch thick. Serve with beans and a stack of warm corn tortillas. **Serves 6.**

basic recipes
and side dishes

The recipes in this chapter relate to several

dishes in this book or should otherwise be

useful in your kitchen.

Asian Slaw

1 large head green
cabbage, about
4-4½ lb.

1 medium red bell
pepper, julienned

6 green onions, green
part only, sliced thin

3 tbsp. chopped ginger

1 tbsp. chopped garlic

2 tbsp. rice vinegar

4 tbsp. mushroom-
flavored soy sauce

1 tbsp. sesame oil

Cut the cabbage in half through the stem. Carefully trim out the
core with a sharp knife. Slice the cabbage thinly on a mandoline
or in a food processor with the slicing disk. In a large bowl, toss
the cabbage together with the remaining ingredients until well
mixed. **Serves 10 to 12.**

Citrus Vinaigrette

Citrus vinaigrettes are healthy and refreshing alternatives to other sauces in the warmer months. Experiment with different ratios of juices. Utilize other citrus as well. Tangerines are excellent, and blood oranges (when you can find them) lend a wonderful red tinge to the vinaigrette. These vinaigrettes are an excellent accompaniment to almost any fish dish.

1 lemon

1 lime

3 oranges

2 grapefruit

3 tbsp. chopped cilantro

2 tbsp. rice vinegar

½ tsp. kosher salt

½ cup olive oil

Squeeze all of the citrus juices into the same bowl, using a strainer to catch the seeds. Add the cilantro, vinegar, and salt. Slowly drizzle in the oil while whisking. **Serves 6.**

Tangerine Vinaigrette

6 tangerines

2 tbsp. minced shallots

1 tbsp. chopped cilantro

¼ cup champagne vinegar

½ tsp. salt

1 cup olive oil

Squeeze the tangerine juice into a bowl, using a strainer to catch the seeds. Add the shallots, cilantro, vinegar, and salt. Slowly drizzle in the oil while whisking. **Serves 6.**

Lobster Vinaigrette

2 large lobsters, 1½-2 lb. each

Ice water

1 shallot, minced

2 tbsp. chopped fresh tarragon

½ tsp. sugar

¼ cup rice vinegar

½ cup olive oil

2 tbsp. extra-virgin olive oil

Kill the lobsters by inserting a knife straight down through the head, right between the eyes. I know this sounds cruel, but given the choice between that and being slowly steamed alive, the knife method seems better. Put 2 inches water into a large stockpot and bring it to a boil. Place the lobsters in the pot on top of a plate or bowl to keep the lobsters raised above the water. Cover the pot tightly and steam the lobsters for 10-12 minutes. Turn off the heat, remove the lobsters with a pair of tongs and shock them in a large bowl of ice water. Keep the lobsters in the ice bath until completely cool.

Remove the lobsters to a cutting board set inside of a baking pan with sides, to prevent lobster juices from running all over the table. Break off the claws and tails. Remove the lobster meat from the shells, using a metal skewer to get out all the hard-to-reach bits. Don't neglect the legs, which have little morsels of meat in them as well. (The payoff for this tedious job is that you get to eat little bites of freshly steamed lobster as you are doing it.) Dice the claw meat and the leg meat. Slice the tails into thin medallions.

In a stainless-steel bowl, place the shallot, tarragon, sugar, and vinegar. Whisk until the sugar dissolves, then whisk in the olive oils. Stir the diced lobster claw and leg meat into the vinaigrette. Portion the sliced tail meat equally among 6 plates, and then ladle the vinaigrette on top. **Serves 6.**

Lobster Vinaigrette with Ginger and Scallions

2 large lobsters, 1½-2
lb. each

Juice of 1 orange

Juice of 1 lime

4 tbsp. rice vinegar

1 tbsp. chopped ginger

1 tsp. chopped
jalapeño pepper

1 tbsp. cilantro "chives"
(chopped cilantro stems)

1 cup olive oil

¼ cup extra-virgin olive
oil

2 green onions, green
part only, sliced

Follow the method for steaming and breaking down lobster in the previous recipe. Place the orange juice, lime juice, vinegar, ginger, jalapeño, and cilantro chives in a stainless-steel bowl. Whisk in the olive oils, and then stir in the green onions. Stir the diced lobster claw and leg meat into the vinaigrette. Portion the sliced tail meat equally among 6 plates, and then ladle the vinaigrette on top. Try this vinaigrette on Cornmeal-Crusted Grouper, Ginger-Steamed Snapper, or Cilantro-Crusted Mahi-Mahi (see index). **Serves 6.**

Lemon-Caper Vinaigrette

Juice of 2 lemons

2 tbsp. capers

½ tsp. kosher salt

1 tsp. minced garlic

2 tbsp. dry white wine

⅔ cup olive oil

1 tbsp. chopped curly-
leaf parsley

½ tsp. fresh-ground
black pepper

Place the lemon juice, capers, salt, garlic, and wine in a stain-less-steel bowl. Whisk in the oil. Stir in the parsley and pepper. This is great with steamed or sautéed snapper. **Serves 6.**

Thai Dipping Sauce with Cucumber and Peanuts

½ cup rice vinegar

¼ cup sugar

½ tsp. salt

½ cup water

1 tbsp. Thai fish sauce

1 red chile, sliced

½ cucumber, peeled
and sliced thin

¼ cup roasted peanuts,
coarsely chopped

Cilantro leaves for
garnish

Simmer the vinegar, sugar, salt, and water together in a saucepan until the sugar and salt are dissolved. Remove from heat and cool. Add the fish sauce and chile. Portion sauce into 4 individual dipping bowls and garnish with the cucumber slices, peanuts, and cilantro. **Serves 4.**

Thai Peanut Sauce

¼ cup rice vinegar

¼ cup water

¼ cup sugar

½ cup smooth peanut butter

1½ tbsp. chopped ginger

2 cloves garlic, minced

2 tbsp. chopped cilantro

½ tsp. crushed red pepper

3 tbsp. soy sauce

1 tbsp. sesame oil

Combine vinegar, water, and sugar in a small saucepan and bring to a boil. Reduce to a simmer and cook for 5 minutes. Remove from heat and cool. Place in blender with peanut butter and puree until smooth. Add ginger, garlic, cilantro, red pepper, soy sauce, and oil and mix well. **Serves 6 to 8.**

Chile-Soy Dipping Sauce

This also makes a great finishing sauce for stir-fried vegetables.

½ cup mushroom-flavored soy sauce

½ cup rice vinegar

1 tsp. crushed red pepper

½ tsp. sesame oil

3 green onions, sliced

Mix together the soy sauce, vinegar, red pepper, and oil and stir. Pour into individual dipping bowls and garnish each bowl with the green onions. **Serves 8 to 10.**

Nuoc Cham

¼ cup rice vinegar

¼ cup soy sauce

1 red chile pepper, sliced thin

2 cloves garlic, minced

Juice of 2 limes

2 tbsp. sugar

Cilantro leaves for garnish

Mix together vinegar, soy sauce, chile, garlic, lime juice, and sugar and stir until sugar dissolves. Garnish with cilantro just before serving. **Serves 6 as a dipping sauce.**

Sweet and Sour Sauce

1 cup water

2 tsp. lemon juice

1 tbsp. orange juice

1 tbsp. chopped ginger

¼ cup sugar

3 tbsp. white-wine vinegar

½ cup ketchup

1 tbsp. cornstarch dissolved in 1 tbsp. cold water

Place the water, lemon juice, orange juice, ginger, sugar, vinegar, and ketchup in a medium saucepan. Bring to a boil, stirring until the sugar dissolves. While the sauce is boiling, slowly drizzle in the cornstarch mixture while stirring. Remove from heat and cool to room temperature before serving. **Serves 6 to 8 as a dipping sauce.**

Dragon Juice

1 cup peanut oil

2 tbsp. crushed red pepper

½ cup sesame oil

Gradually heat the peanut oil in a saucepan over medium heat. Add the red pepper and remove from heat. Allow the oil to cool completely, then strain, discarding the red pepper. Add the sesame oil. Store in a clean glass jar. It will keep indefinitely.

Green Chile Sauce

4 jalapeño peppers,
steamed and seeded

1 bunch cilantro, stems
and leaves, coarsely
chopped

2 cloves garlic

½ yellow onion, coarsely
chopped

2 tbsp. olive oil

1 tbsp. rice vinegar

Place all ingredients in blender and puree until smooth. Stop the
machine to scrape down the sides with a rubber spatula when
necessary. **Makes about 1½ cups.**

Cilantro Pesto

1 bunch cilantro, rinsed
in cold water and
coarsely chopped

¼ cup toasted
macadamia nuts

1 clove garlic, minced

¼ cup grated Parmesan
cheese

Juice of 1 lemon

½ cup olive oil

Salt to taste

Place all ingredients into a blender and turn it on. Stop occasionally to scrape down the sides. Puree until smooth and set aside
until ready to use. This can be made a day in advance, but it's so
easy why would you? It also freezes beautifully, so if you have a
lot of cilantro on hand, make a big batch and save it for a rainy
day. **Makes about 1½ cups.**

Sage Pesto

½ cup packed fresh sage leaves

Boiling salted water

Ice water

1 clove garlic, minced

Juice of 1 lemon

¾ cup toasted walnuts

⅓ cup grated Parmesan cheese

½ cup packed raw spinach leaves

1 cup olive oil

Salt to taste

Blanch sage leaves for 10 seconds in boiling salted water. Immediately shock in ice water. Chop the sage coarsely and place in blender along with garlic, lemon juice, walnuts, cheese, and spinach. (Blanching the sage and adding spinach to the pesto will give the sauce a nice, green color.) Add the oil and puree until smooth, scraping down the sides of the blender when necessary. Season with salt. **Makes about 1½ cups.**

Black Beans

2 cups dried black beans

½ cup diced yellow onion

2 tbsp. olive oil

½ tsp. cayenne pepper

2 tsp. ground cumin

1 tbsp. chili powder

2 tsp. ground coriander

10 cups water

Salt to taste

Pick through the beans and rinse. Cook the onions in the oil until soft. Add the cayenne pepper, cumin, chili powder, and coriander. Cook the spices, stirring, for about 30 seconds, then add the water and beans. Bring to a boil, reduce to a simmer, and cook for about 1 hour. Season with salt and simmer, stirring occasionally, for an additional 10 minutes. **Makes about 5 cups.**

White Beans

2 cups dried navy beans

½ cup diced yellow onion

2 tbsp. olive oil

2 tbsp. ground coriander

10 cups water

Salt and pepper to taste

Pick through the beans and rinse. Cook the onions in the oil until soft. Add the ground coriander and cook for 30 seconds, stirring. Add the water and beans and bring to a boil. Reduce to a simmer and cook for about 1 hour. Season with salt and pepper. **Makes about 5 cups.**

Cilantro Rice

1 cup basmati rice

½ cup diced yellow onion

2 tbsp. olive oil

1½ cups cold water

1 cup chopped cilantro, stems and leaves

8 tbsp. unsalted butter

Salt to taste

Rinse the rice in several changes of cold water. In a medium saucepan, cook the onions in the oil until soft. Add the rice and stir, then add the water. Bring to a boil, reduce heat to a bare simmer, and cover with a tight-fitting lid. Cook for 15-20 minutes and turn off the heat. Allow the rice to sit, covered, for 5 minutes.

Place the chopped cilantro in a blender. Melt the butter over medium heat and add it to the blender. Puree for 30 seconds on high speed. Place the cooked rice in a large stainless-steel bowl. Add the warm cilantro butter and gently fold it into the rice using a large rubber spatula. Season with salt. This rice holds its shape well. To serve you may fill 4 small cups or ramekins with the warm rice and invert them onto 4 plates. **Serves 4.**

Basic Recipes and Side Dishes   167

Chile-Lime Dipping Sauce

Juice of 5 limes
2 tsp. sugar
4 tbsp. sambal
2 tbsp. rice vinegar
½ tsp. fish sauce

Place the lime juice and sugar in a stainless-steel bowl and stir until the sugar dissolves. Add the remaining ingredients and stir well. This is great with Curried Vegetable Egg Rolls, Pork and Shrimp Lumpia, or Spicy Chicken Lumpia (see index). **Makes about 1 cup.**

Wasabi Pasta Dough

2½ cups all-purpose flour
1 cup wasabi powder
1 tsp. salt
5 eggs
2 tsp. sesame oil

Sift together the flour, wasabi powder, and salt. Mound the dry ingredients on a clean work surface and make a well in the center. Place the eggs and oil into the well. With a fork, begin whipping the eggs, gradually incorporating some of the flour. Continue whipping and incorporating flour until the dough begins to form. Incorporate the remaining flour by hand and knead the dough until smooth. Roll dough into a thin sheet and cut into circles with a round cookie cutter to make your own potsticker wrappers. **Makes about 1½ lb. dough.**

Wasabi Mashed Potatoes

3 Idaho potatoes,
peeled
1 cup milk
4 tbsp. unsalted butter
2 tbsp. wasabi paste
Salt to taste

Cut the potatoes in half lengthwise and place them in a saucepan of cold water. Bring to a boil, reduce to simmer, and cook until potatoes are easily pierced with a knife. Drain the potatoes, return them to the pan, and "steam" them dry by placing the pan back on the stove for a few seconds.

Heat the milk and butter together until the butter melts. Pour over the potatoes and mash together. Gently fold in the wasabi paste with a rubber spatula until well incorporated. Season with salt. **Serves 6.**

Wasabi Aioli

2 tbsp. wasabi powder
2 tbsp. water
¼ tsp. salt
¼ tsp. sesame oil
2 egg yolks
½ tsp. rice vinegar
½ tsp. soy sauce
½ cup peanut oil

Mix the wasabi powder and water together into a smooth paste in a medium stainless-steel bowl. Add salt, sesame oil, egg yolks, vinegar, and soy sauce and stir well. Slowly drizzle in the peanut oil while whisking. Use as a dipping sauce for Crispy Calamari or on Tuna Carpaccio (see index).

Chicken Stock

1 whole chicken, 2½-3 lb.

5 qt. water

2 yellow onions, cut into eighths

1 carrot, peeled and cut into 1-inch pieces

2 ribs celery, cut into 1-inch pieces

2 tbsp. salt

1 bulb garlic, halved

1 bunch green onions, cut into 2-inch pieces

½ cup coarsely chopped ginger

Place all ingredients in a stockpot and bring to a boil. Reduce heat to a bare simmer and cook for 1½ hours. Use a ladle to skim the scum off the top while the stock is simmering. Strain through a fine sieve and cool to room temperature before putting in the refrigerator. Once it is cold, you can remove the congealed fat from the top before using the stock. **Makes about 1 gal.**

5 qt. water

1 bunch celery, cut into ½-inch pieces

3 carrots, peeled and cut into ½-inch pieces

6 yellow onions, coarsely chopped

½ bunch parsley

12 sprigs fresh or 1 tbsp. dried thyme

1 bay leaf

1 tbsp. salt

Place all ingredients in a stockpot and bring to a boil. Reduce to a simmer and cook for 45 minutes to 1 hour. Strain and cool to room temperature before storing in the refrigerator. **Makes about 1 gal.**

Corn and Black Bean Salsa

Kernels from 5 ears fresh sweet corn

Boiling salted water

2 cups cooked black beans, rinsed (see index)

½ cup diced red onion

4 tbsp. diced red bell pepper

Juice of 1 lime

1 clove garlic, minced

2 tbsp. chopped cilantro

1 small jalapeño pepper, seeded and chopped

½ tsp. ground toasted cumin seed

2 tbsp. olive oil

Salt and fresh-ground black pepper to taste

Cook corn in the water 5 minutes. Drain and cool. In a stainless-steel bowl, mix the corn with the beans, onion, bell pepper, lime juice, garlic, cilantro, jalapeño, and cumin. Mix well, and then stir in the oil. Season with salt and pepper. This is great with grilled fish or chicken. **Serves 6.**

1 lb. fresh tomatillos

1 serrano pepper, minced

Juice of 1 lime

½ red onion, diced small

2 tbsp. chopped cilantro

1 tbsp. extra-virgin olive oil

Salt and fresh-ground black pepper to taste

Remove the husks from the tomatillos, if any, and rinse tomatillos well in cold water. Carefully remove the stem ends with a sharp paring knife. Slice the tomatillos, and then chop fairly finely. Put the chopped tomatillos in a fine sieve and let them drain off excess liquid. Once the tomatillos are well drained, mix them in a stainless-steel bowl with the serrano pepper, lime juice, onion, cilantro, and oil. Season with salt and pepper. **Serves 6 to 8.**

Papaya Salsa

1 ripe papaya

3 tbsp. chopped cilantro

1 jalapeño pepper, minced

Juice of 1 lime

2 tbsp. coriander seeds

Peel, seed, and dice the papaya. In a stainless-steel bowl, toss the papaya with the cilantro, jalapeño, and lime juice. Toast the coriander seeds in a dry skillet over medium heat until the seeds are aromatic and smoking slightly. Grind the seeds in a spice grinder or with a mortar and pestle, then sift them through a fine sieve and discard the husks. Add the ground coriander to the salsa and mix well. **Serves 4 to 6.**

desserts

Because I like to finish a meal on a light note, I have included many recipes for simple fruit sorbets and ice creams. Most of the desserts in this chapter are quite simple and can be made ahead of time. There are some classic desserts with a Pacific Rim twist as well.

Chocolate-Banana Lumpia

Chocolate-Banana Lumpia

Lumpia is the Filipino version of the egg roll. I gleaned this recipe from some of the Filipino women I worked with in Hawaii. On slow nights, the "pantry ladies" would roll up a bunch of these and we would eat them, sprinkled with powdered sugar, as fast as they could make them.

6 ripe bananas

12 egg-roll wrappers

½ lb. semisweet chocolate, chopped

1 tbsp. flour mixed with 1 tbsp. water to make a "slurry"

Peanut oil for frying

Powdered sugar for garnish

Peel the bananas and cut in half lengthwise, then crosswise. Lay 1 egg-roll wrapper on a clean, flat work surface with one corner pointing towards you. Place 1 banana slice in the middle of the wrapper with the cut side up. Top the banana with about 1 oz. chocolate. Place the corresponding slice of banana on top. Roll the lumpia by starting with the corner nearest you and folding it over the banana. Roll halfway, fold in the two side corners, and continue rolling until only a small corner of the egg-roll wrapper is exposed. Brush the corner with a dab of the slurry and seal the lumpia. Continue with remaining bananas.

Fry the lumpia until golden brown in 350-degree oil. Sprinkle with powdered sugar and serve immediately. **Makes 12 lumpia.**

Tart Dough

2 cups all-purpose flour

1 tsp. salt

2 tsp. sugar

½ lb. chilled unsalted butter, cut into tbsp.-size cubes

¼ cup ice water

Put flour, salt, and sugar in a food processor with the blade attachment. Pulse until well blended. Add the cold butter and pulse until the mixture resembles coarse crumbs.

With the machine running, slowly drizzle in the ice water until the dough forms and comes away from the sides of the machine. You may not need all of the water. Immediately stop the machine and remove the dough. On a lightly floured surface, gently form the dough into a thick disk. Wrap in plastic and allow to rest in refrigerator for at least 30 minutes.

Mango Curd Tart

1 recipe Tart Dough
1 cup granulated sugar
1 cup heavy whipping cream
4 eggs
7 oz. mango puree (see below)
2 tbsp. fresh-squeezed lime juice

Roll the dough out on a lightly floured surface to ⅛ inch thick. Place dough in a buttered and floured 10½-inch tart pan. Line the top of the tart with parchment paper or wax paper. Fill the tart pan with dried beans, rice, or some other pie weights. Bake in a preheated 350-degree oven until the crust is golden brown around the edges, about 15 minutes. Remove the pie weights and return the tart shell to the oven for an additional 4-5 minutes. Remove from the oven and cool.

Place sugar and cream in a small saucepan and bring to a boil, stirring, until sugar dissolves. Remove from heat and cool. Whisk together the eggs, mango puree, and lime juice until well blended. Fold in the cooled cream mixture. Pour into prebaked tart shell and bake in a preheated 350-degree oven for 30 minutes or until the filling is set. **Serves 8.**

Canned mango puree can be found in Mediterranean markets. To make mango puree, peel and seed 2 very ripe mangos and puree in blender with 4 tbsp. water.

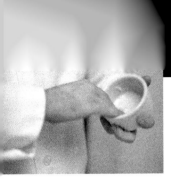

Tart

1 recipe Tart Dough

2 cups fresh cooked pumpkin puree

¼ cup heavy whipping cream

2 eggs

½ cup light brown sugar

½ cup granulated sugar

¼ cup cake flour

1 tsp. vanilla extract

1 tbsp. Chinese five-spice powder

1 tsp. cinnamon

1 tsp. nutmeg

Ginger-Caramel Sauce

⅓ cup granulated sugar

1 cup water

1 cup heavy whipping cream

1 tbsp. chopped ginger

Crème Anglaise (see index)

Roll out the dough into a buttered and floured 10½-inch tart pan. Line the top of the tart with parchment paper or wax paper and fill the pan with dried beans, rice, or some other pie weights. Bake in a preheated 350-degree oven until the crust is golden brown around the edges, about 15 minutes. Remove the pie weights and return the tart shell to the oven for an additional 4-5 minutes. Remove from the oven and cool.

Place the remaining tart ingredients in a large bowl and stir until well mixed. Pour into prebaked tart shell and bake in a preheated 350-degree oven for 30-40 minutes or until a toothpick inserted in the center comes out clean.

To make the sauce, place the sugar and water in a heavy, thick-bottomed saucepan. Slowly heat the mixture, swirling the pan until the sugar dissolves. Avoid stirring, which could cause the sugar to crystallize. Once all of the sugar has dissolved, bring to a boil and cover the pan with a tight-fitting lid. Cook for several minutes, covered, until the sugar begins to darken. Remove the lid and continue cooking the sugar and swirling the pan until it turns a nice caramel color. Remove from the heat and allow to cool slightly. Add the cream and return to the heat. Stir until the sauce turns smooth. Remove from heat and stir in the ginger. Allow to cool completely or keep warm until ready to serve.

Cut the tart into 8 slices. Ladle an ounce or so of Crème Anglaise on each plate, and top with a slice of tart. Drizzle with the caramel sauce. **Serves 8.**

Crème Brûlée

Literally "burnt cream," the French and the English both claim this ubiquitous dessert as their own. Wherever it originated, it has found its way onto the menu of nearly every upscale restaurant in the country. There are many variations of the recipe, but all of them call for the same basic ingredients: cream, sugar, eggs, and vanilla.

I have, over the years, experimented with different variations on the crème brûlée theme, but I keep coming back to the standard. If it ain't broke, don't fix it. Some crème brûlée recipes call for browning the sugar-crusted custards in the broiler of your oven, but for me, there is no better method (for results or pure showmanship) than a propane blowtorch. Being able to caramelize crème brûlées in front of your friends at your next dinner party is justification enough for buying one.

12 egg yolks
1 cup granulated sugar
1 qt. heavy whipping cream
1 vanilla bean
¾ cup turbinado sugar

Place the egg yolks in a large, stainless-steel bowl. Put the sugar and cream into a saucepan. Cut the vanilla bean in half lengthwise and, using the backside of a paring knife, scrape out the tiny black seeds from the bean pod. Put the scrapings and the bean pod into the saucepan with the sugar and cream.

Bring the mixture to a boil, stirring until the sugar dissolves. Pluck out the bean pod with a pair of tongs and set aside. (Allow the pod to dry completely, then store in an airtight container with granulated sugar. The sugar will pick up some of the vanilla flavor.) Carefully ladle 1 cup or so of the hot mixture into the egg yolks while whisking. Pour in the remaining hot mixture while whisking. Strain through a fine sieve to remove any bits of cooked egg.

Place 6 shallow, ovenproof dishes in a level baking pan with sides. Carefully ladle the crème brûlée mixture evenly into the dishes. Place the pan in a preheated 300-degree oven. Pour hot water into the pan until it reaches about halfway up the sides of the dishes. Bake for 45 minutes or until the custard is still just a tad bit jiggly when you shake the pan. Carefully remove the pan from the oven and allow the custards to sit until cool enough to handle. Remove them from the pan into a dry pan and store them in the refrigerator until you are ready to serve them.

To serve, make sure that the custards are free of any excess moisture on top. Dab them with a paper towel if necessary. Sprinkle each custard with about 2 tbsp. turbinado sugar. Smooth the sugar out so that it evenly covers the entire surface of the custard. Pour off any excess sugar. With a back and forth motion, apply the torch to the sugar on top of the custards until each one is a golden, caramelized color. Allow the brûlées to sit for a few minutes until the crust hardens. **Serves 6.**

Crème Anglaise

This French term means "English cream." It makes you think that the English have proprietary rights to crème brûlée after all, since the recipes are very similar. If the plate is the pastry chef's canvas, then crème anglaise is the paint—or one of them, anyway. This recipe can be adapted to individual tastes or purposes by substituting a different liqueur. Crème anglaise is used as a sauce or garnish on a wide range of desserts.

5 egg yolks

2 tsp. vanilla extract

2 tbsp. Grand Marnier (or liqueur of your choice)

1½ cups milk

¼ cup sugar

Ice water

Place egg yolks, vanilla, and Grand Marnier in blender. Bring milk and sugar to a boil in a heavy saucepan. With the blender running, pour the hot milk mixture into the egg mixture. Return the liquid to the saucepan and put it back on the stove over medium heat. Stir constantly until the sauce begins to bubble around the edges and thicken. Immediately strain through a fine sieve into a stainless-steel bowl set inside of another stainless-steel bowl filled with ice water. Stir until completely cool. Funnel into a squeeze bottle and store in the refrigerator for up to 3 days.

Ginger Ice

This is a perfect yin and yang experience for the taste buds: cool, pungent, sweet, sour. The ginger retains its bite but balances well with the sweetness and the lime juice. You may freeze this in an ice-cream freezer for a much smoother sorbet, but you will dull the effects of the ginger by doing so.

2½ cups sugar
5 cups water
½ cup coarsely chopped ginger
Juice of 3 limes

Bring the sugar and water to boil while stirring. Reduce heat and simmer for 5 minutes. Remove from heat and add ginger. Allow to steep for 15 minutes, then strain. Add lime juice and allow to cool completely. Pour into a shallow baking pan and place on a level surface in the freezer. Allow to freeze overnight.

To serve, use the tines of a fork to scrape the surface of the ice until you build up enough shavings for a scoop. Serve in a chilled martini glass. **Makes about 1½ qt.**

For a Pacific Rim martini: Fill a cocktail shaker half-full with cracked ice. Add 2 oz. of your favorite vodka and shake well. Strain into a chilled martini glass and garnish with a small scoop of ginger ice. This is an "up" martini that stays chilled while you drink it and finishes with a great fresh-ginger kick.

Simple Syrup

Simple syrup can be used as a base for a nearly inexhaustible array of sorbets. It can also be used as a sweetener for cocktails and iced tea and as a base for lemonade. Once made, simple syrup can be stored indefinitely in the refrigerator.

5 cups sugar
4½ cups water

Mix sugar and water together in a saucepan. Bring to boil while stirring. Boil until sugar dissolves and mixture turns clear. Cool before using. Store in a clean covered jar in the refrigerator. **Makes about 1 qt.**

Lemongrass Elixir

5 cups water
5 cups sugar
½ cup chopped lemon-grass

Place the sugar and water in a heavy saucepan. Bring to a boil, stirring until the sugar dissolves. Reduce to a simmer and cook for 3 minutes. Add the chopped lemongrass to the sugar water. Cover and allow to cool completely. Strain and discard lemon-grass. Try the following serving suggestions. Toss fresh strawberries or other fruit with a few tablespoons of elixir and serve over Vanilla-Bean Ice Cream. Use it as a sweetener for iced tea. Pour some on the rocks with a splash of soda water. Use in place of simple syrup in your favorite cocktail recipes. **Makes about 1 qt.**

Sorbet Variations

Sorbets are a wonderful finish to a summer meal. Your options are only limited by the ingredients you can get. I find citrus-based sorbets the most refreshing. However, a great sorbet can be made out of practically anything your desire. I have made a jalapeño sorbet as a garnish for chilled watermelon soup. I have made a gazpacho sorbet to garnish a chilled avocado soup. I even (jokingly) made a curry sorbet as a palate cleanser for a wine dinner hosted at Tsunami. It ended up being the most talked-about course of the evening. What I mean is, people actually *enjoyed* it.

The following sorbet ratios can be tweaked to suit your personal tastes. Here are a few rules of thumb to go by.

Just because a fruit is sweet to the taste does not mean it won't need additional sugar. Freezing tends to dull sweetness.

A high sugar content gives sorbet a smooth texture and prevents ice crystals from forming. However, too much sugar will prevent the sorbet from freezing at all.

The addition of a small amount of alcohol will also inhibit ice crystallization. Likewise, excessive amounts of alcohol will prevent freezing altogether. If you want the *flavor* of your favorite distilled beverage, you can burn off the alcohol before adding it to your sorbet recipe.

A simple test for the proper ratio of sugar syrup to fruit juice in a sorbet is the egg test. Drop a whole, raw egg (shell on, of course) in your fruit juice and simple syrup mixture. When the ideal sugar level is reached, a quarter-sized portion of the egg will be exposed. Adjust the fruit puree or the simple syrup accordingly.

To make any sorbet smoother, fold in one egg white (whipped to soft peaks) for every quart of sorbet just before it is completely frozen.

Cantaloupe Sorbet

**1 ripe cantaloupe,
peeled and seeded**

1 cup simple syrup

Puree the cantaloupe in a blender until smooth. Mix the cantaloupe puree with the simple syrup and freeze in an ice-cream maker. **Makes about 1 qt.**

Grapefruit Sorbet

**3 cup fresh-squeezed
grapefruit juice**

¾ cup simple syrup

Mix the grapefruit juice and simple syrup together and freeze in ice-cream maker. **Makes about 1 qt.**

1 cup sugar

½ cup water

Juice of 1 lemon

Zest of 4 lemons

1 cup fresh-squeezed lemon juice

Juice of 1 lime

2 cups sparkling mineral water

1 cup dry white wine

Combine the sugar, water, and juice of 1 lemon in a saucepan and bring to a boil, stirring. Reduce to a simmer and cook until the sugar is dissolved and the mixture turns clear. Remove from heat and cool completely.

Add the lemon zest, 1 cup lemon juice, lime juice, mineral water, and wine and mix well. Freeze in ice-cream maker. **Makes just over 1 qt.**

Champagne-Lime Sorbet

1½ cups simple syrup

1½ cups fresh-squeezed lime juice

1½ cups champagne or sparkling wine

Combine all ingredients and freeze in ice-cream maker. **Makes about 1 qt.**

Lemongrass Sorbet

1½ cups sugar
3 cups water
1 cup minced lemongrass, white part only
Juice of 2 limes

Bring the sugar and water to a boil, stirring until the sugar dissolves. Remove from heat, add the lemongrass, and allow it to steep, covered, for 15 minutes. Strain the lemongrass out and add the lime juice. Allow to cool completely before freezing in ice-cream maker. **Makes about 1 qt.**

Plum Sorbet

1½ cups sugar
1½ cups water
2 lb. plums, halved and pitted
Juice of 1 lemon

Bring the sugar and water to a boil, stirring until sugar dissolves. Add the plums and simmer until tender. Remove from the heat and cool. Puree the plums and liquid, then strain through a fine sieve. Add the lemon juice. Freeze in ice-cream maker. **Makes about 1 qt.**

Clockwise from left: Cantaloupe Sorbet,
Lemongrass Sorbet, Plum Sorbet

Apple Sorbet

4 Fuji or Pink Lady
apples, cored
2 cups sugar
2 cups water
Juice of 3 lemons

Quarter the apples and place them in a saucepan with the sugar and water. Bring to a boil, stirring until the sugar dissolves. Reduce to a simmer and cook for 8-10 minutes or until the apples begin to soften. Add the lemon juice. Puree the mixture, then strain and cool completely. Freeze in ice-cream maker.
Makes about 1 qt.

Mango Sorbet

1½ cups mango puree
Juice of 1 lime
½ cup simple syrup
½ cup water

Mix all ingredients together and freeze in ice-cream maker.
Makes about 1 pt.

Pineapple Sorbet

½ pineapple, peeled
and cubed

Juice of 2 lemons

2½ cups simple syrup

Puree pineapple in blender along with the lemon juice. Remove to a stainless-steel bowl, add the simple syrup, and stir well. Freeze in ice-cream maker. **Makes about 1½ qt.**

Cinnamon-Honey Ice Cream

8 egg yolks

2 cups half-and-half

2 cups heavy whipping
cream

1 cup honey

1 tbsp. ground
cinnamon

Place the egg yolks in a stainless-steel bowl. Combine half-and-half, cream, honey, and cinnamon in a heavy saucepan and bring to a boil. Pour 1 cup of the hot liquid over the egg yolks while whisking. Mix well and scrape the egg-yolk mixture back into the saucepan with a rubber spatula.

Return to the stove over medium heat. Cook, stirring constantly, until the mixture thickens enough to coat the back of a spoon. Cool, then freeze in ice-cream maker. **Makes about 1 qt.**

Vanilla-Bean Ice Cream

2 vanilla beans
1 qt. half-and-half
2 cups sugar
14 egg yolks
1 qt. heavy whipping cream

Split the vanilla beans in half lengthwise and scrape out the seeds from each half. Place the scrapings and pods in a saucepan along with the half-and-half and sugar. Bring to a boil, stirring until the sugar dissolves.

Place the egg yolks in a stainless-steel bowl. Ladle 1 cup of the hot liquid into the egg yolks while whisking. Strain the egg-yolk mixture back into the saucepan and discard the vanilla bean.

Return the pan to the stove. Cook over medium heat, stirring constantly, until the mixture begins to thicken. Remove from heat and add the cream.

Allow mixture to cool completely before freezing in an ice-cream maker. For best results, allow the mixture to sit in the refrigerator overnight before freezing. **Makes just over 2 qt.**

Lemongrass Ice Cream

7 egg yolks

2 cups half-and-half

1 cup chopped fresh lemongrass

1 cup sugar

1 vanilla bean

2 cups heavy whipping cream

Put the eggs in a stainless-steel bowl. Place the half-and-half, lemongrass, and sugar into a heavy saucepan. Split the vanilla bean lengthwise and scrape the seeds out using the backside of a paring knife. Put the scrapings along with the pod in the saucepan. Bring the liquid to a boil over medium-high heat, stirring until the sugar dissolves.

Pour 1 cup of the hot liquid over the egg yolks while whisking. Mix well and scrape the mixture back into the saucepan with a rubber spatula. Return the pan to the stove and cook over medium heat, stirring constantly, until the mixture thickens enough to coat the back of a spoon. Remove from heat. Remove the pod and add the cream.

For best results, allow the mixture to sit in the refrigerator overnight. Then freeze in ice-cream maker. **Makes about 1 qt.**

Avocado Ice Cream

1 qt. milk
1½ cups sugar
6 egg yolks
3 ripe avocados

Bring milk and sugar to a boil in a medium saucepan, stirring until sugar dissolves. Whisk the hot liquid into the egg yolks in a stainless-steel bowl. Return the mixture to the saucepan and cook over medium heat, stirring constantly, until the sauce is thick enough to coat the back of a spoon. Pour the mixture into a clean stainless-steel bowl and allow to cool completely.

Peel and pit the avocados. Add the avocados to the ice-cream base and then puree the mixture in a blender until smooth. Freeze in ice-cream maker. **Makes about 1½ qt.**

Strawberry Ice Cream

1 qt. half-and-half
1½ cups sugar
6 egg yolks
2 lb. strawberries, hulled

Bring half-and-half and sugar to a boil in a heavy saucepan, stirring until sugar dissolves. Whisk the hot liquid into the egg yolks in a stainless-steel bowl. Return the mixture to the saucepan and cook over medium heat, stirring constantly, until thick enough to coat the back of a spoon. Pour the mixture into a clean stainless-steel bowl and allow to cool. Place in a blender with the berries and puree until smooth. Freeze in ice-cream maker. **Makes about 2 qt.**

*Clockwise from top: Avocado Ice Cream,
Vanilla-Bean Ice Cream, Cinnamon-
Honey Ice Cream, Strawberry Ice Cream*

Mango Ice Cream

8 egg yolks
1 cup sugar
1 qt. half-and-half
1 tbsp. vanilla extract
Ice water
1½ cups mango puree
½ cup diced mango

Mix egg yolks and sugar together well. Bring the half-and-half to a boil in a medium saucepan. Pour the hot liquid into the egg mixture while whisking.

Return the mixture to the saucepan over medium heat and cook, stirring constantly, until the custard thickens enough to coat the back of a spoon. Strain the mixture through a fine sieve into a stainless-steel bowl. Add vanilla. Place the bowl into a larger stainless-steel bowl filled with ice water and stir the mixture until cool.

Stir in the mango puree and diced mango. Allow the mixture to cool in the refrigerator for at least 4 hours before freezing in ice-cream maker. **Makes about 2 qt.**

Mojito Rum Cakes

My wife adapted this dessert from an old family recipe. We had been drinking mojitos, a refreshing rum and lime cocktail laced with fresh mint, when Colleen said something like, "Wouldn't it be great if you could capture this flavor in a dessert?" Next thing I know, she's off to the kitchen with a bottle of rum, some mint, a bunch of limes, and her family recipe for rum cake. What she ended up with is one of our best-selling desserts.

2⅔ cups all-purpose flour

2¼ tsp. baking powder

½ tsp. salt

½ lb. unsalted butter

1½ cups sugar plus ¼ cup sugar

4 egg yolks

4 egg whites

¾ cup rum

½ cup heavy whipping cream

Glaze

½ cup unsalted butter

2 cups sugar

½ cup water

¾ cup rum

Zest and juice of 1 lime

2 tbsp. chopped fresh mint

Sift together the flour, baking powder, and salt. Whip the butter and 1½ cups sugar together until fluffy. Whip in the egg yolks one at a time. Remove to a large stainless-steel bowl. Beat the egg whites to stiff peaks with ¼ cup sugar. Mix the rum with the cream. Fold ⅓ of the dry ingredients into the butter mixture with a rubber spatula. Fold in ⅓ of the rum mixture. Continue to alternately fold the dry and wet ingredients into the batter until incorporated. Gently fold in the beaten egg whites. Butter and flour 12 8-oz. ovenproof ramekins. Fill each ramekin ⅔ full and bake in a 350-degree oven for 25-30 minutes.

To make the glaze, place the butter, sugar, and water in a small saucepan and bring to a boil. Reduce the heat and simmer the mixture for 5 minutes. Remove from the heat and add the rum, lime zest, lime juice, and mint. Allow to cool slightly.

When the cakes are done baking, remove from the oven and allow them to cool in the ramekins for 20 minutes. With a serrated knife, slice the top off each cake so that they are level. While the glaze is still warm, ladle evenly over each cake. Allow the cakes to cool completely before removing them from the ramekins. **Makes 12 individual cakes.**

Mixed Berries with Sake Sabayon

This dessert originated in Italy, where it is know as *zabaglione*. It is a mixture of egg yolks, sugar, and wine (traditionally Marsala), which is whipped over simmering water. The result is a light, foamy custard that is great over fresh fruit or cake. I have given this classic dessert a Pacific Rim spin by using sake and *mirin*, a sweet Japanese cooking wine made from glutinous rice. *Mirin* can be found in Asian markets.

6 egg yolks

½ cup *mirin*

½ cup sake

⅓ cup sugar

1 tsp. lemon juice

3 pt. mixed berries (blueberries, strawberries, blackberries)

Place the egg yolks, *mirin*, sake, sugar, and lemon juice in a stainless-steel bowl. The sabayon will expand as it cooks, so choose a bowl that will allow for that. Place the bowl over a pot of water at a low simmer. Make sure the bowl nestles down into the pot but does not touch the water. Whisk continually until the mixture triples in volume. Once the sabayon is cooked, you may serve it warm, or cool it down and serve it chilled. (If you cool it down it will lose some volume.)

Place a spoonful of the mixed berries in each of 6 white-wine glasses. Top with a ladle of the sabayon, then another spoonful of berries. Top the glasses off with the remaining sabayon. Serve immediately or keep in refrigerator to serve later. **Serves 6.**

Plum Crisp with Lemongrass

2½ lb. ripe plums

3 tbsp. granulated sugar

1 cup flour

½ cup light brown sugar

¼ cup granulated sugar

½ tsp. Chinese five-spice powder

3 tbsp. minced lemon grass

8 tbsp. cold unsalted butter, cut into chunks

¾ cup macadamia nuts, coarsely chopped

Pit and slice the plums and toss them with the 3 tbsp. granulated sugar. Fill 8 8-oz. ovenproof ramekins ¾ full with the plums. Place the flour, brown sugar, ¼ cup granulated sugar, Chinese five-spice powder, and lemongrass in the bowl of a food processor and pulse the machine until the ingredients are well mixed. Add the cold butter pieces to the flour mixture and pulse the machine until the dough resembles coarse meal.

Remove the dough to a stainless-steel bowl and fold in the macadamia nuts by hand. Top each of the ramekins with the dough. Place on a cookie sheet and bake in a preheated 425-degree oven 20-25 minutes or until bubbling around the edges. Serve with a scoop of Cinnamon-Honey or Vanilla-Bean Ice Cream (see index). **Serves 8.**

index